PRECALCULUS MATHEMATICS
A Graphing Approach
Third Edition

Gregory D. Foley *Sam Houston State University*

Linda Taylor *University of Cincinnati*

Addison-Wesley Publishing Company

Menlo Park, California • Reading, Massachusetts • New York • Don Mills, Ontario
Wokingham, England • Amsterdam • Bonn • Sydney • Singapore • Tokyo
Madrid • San Juan • Paris • Seoul, Korea • Milan • Mexico City • Taipei, Taiwan

ISBN 0-201-86143-7

1 2 3 4 5 6 7 8 9 10-ML-97 96 95 94 93

CONTENTS

Using Graphing Calculators In Assessment

As with the philosophy of *Precalculus Mathematics: A Graphing Approach*, the tests in this publication are designed with the assumption that students have access to graphing calculators. It is further assumed that students will have the calculators on their desks as they take each test. There are, however, many problems that do not require the use of a graphing calculator.

Research has shown that students who have used technology in their study of mathematics have a deep understanding of the mathematical principles and concepts. Even when students who are accustomed to using technology are denied access to calculators during tests, they test as well or better than students who have never used technology (Hembree & Dessart, 1986).

The tests in this publication have three types of problems: (1) *calculator specific*, in which the use of a graphing calculator is necessary for the solution; (2) *calculator neutral*, in which the graphing calculator could be used but the problem can be solved without it; and (3) *calculator inactive*, in which a graphing calculator will be of no use (Kenelly, 1990). Since students studying from *Precalculus Mathematics: A Graphing Approach* will have had many experiences with these types of problems, they will be prepared for the types of problems found on the tests.

Hembree, Ray, & Dessart, Donald J. (1986). Effects of hand-held calculators in precollege mathematics education: A meta-analysis. *Journal for Research in Mathematics Education*, 17, 83–99.

Kenelly, John. (1990). Using calculators in the standardized testing of mathematics. *Mathematics Teacher*, 83, 716–720.

Alternative Assessments

Chapter 1

Group Activity

Explore the general form of quadratic equations $y = ax^2 + bx + c$. Make some conjectures about the coefficients a, b, and c, and the differences in the graphs when the coefficients are changed.

Student Log (or Journal)

Compare the discussion of parallel and perpendicular lines in this chapter with the definitions and theorems about parallel and perpendicular lines discussed in geometry class.

Open-ended Question

Find a subset of the real numbers that has commutative and associative properties but does not have closure. Demonstrate each of these characteristics.

Chapter 2

Group Activity

The long sides of a rectangular sheet of metal are folded up to form a rain gutter. The objective is to form a gutter with the maximum cross-sectional area from a sheet of metal of a specific size. Is this how gutters are really made? Do real gutters have both sides equal? Do all gutters have a rectangular cross-section? Is there a more efficient shape for carrying water?

Student Log (or Journal)

Describe how you determine that the graph of a function is a *complete* graph. Indicate the various concepts you consider when making your decision.

Open-ended Question

Find a complete graph of $y = \frac{1}{3}x^3 + 5x^2 - 2$. Give reasons for knowing that you have a complete graph of the function.

Chapter 3

Group Activity

Find the meaning of the words *period, sidereal period, synodic period, posigrade orbit*, and *retrograde orbit*. (Hint: The words all relate to the orbits of spacecraft and planets.) The sidereal period, P, (in seconds) is given by the formula

$$P = 2\pi\sqrt{\frac{a^3}{GM}}$$

where a is the average radius of orbit from the center of the body about which the satellite is in motion, G is the constant of universal gravitation, and M is the mass of the body about which the satellite orbits.

Find the sidereal period of the *High Energy Astronomy Observatory (HEAO)* satellites, which have an average altitude above Earth of 430 km. The average radius of Earth is 6370 km, and the value of the product GM for Earth is 3.99×10^{14} $m^3/\sec^2$. (Problem found in Kastner, B. (1985). *Space Mathematics*. Reston, VA: NCTM.)

Student Log (or Journal)

In your own words, describe a complex number.

Open-ended Question

Why do we need to be able to find all extreme values of a function? Why do we need to be able to find the zeros of a function? Why do we want to know the intervals over which a function is increasing and decreasing?

Chapter 4

Group Activity

In Section 4.4, a generalization about how the odd/even nature of n influenced the graphs of $y = \sqrt[n]{x}$ was made. Make similar conjectures if x is raised to a fractional power, such as $\frac{2}{3}, \frac{3}{4}, \frac{4}{5}, \ldots$. What is the effect upon the graphs of $y = \sqrt[3]{x}$, $y = \sqrt[4]{x}$, and $y = \sqrt[5]{x}$, $\ldots$, respectively, for instance.

Student Log (or Journal)

Why is it important to identify the values of the variable(s) that cause the denominator of a rational function to be zero?

Open-ended Question

Parcels of land for homes in a rural county are being sold in 1-acre (43,560 ft^2) portions. If you wanted to fence your lot, you would want the one with the minimum perimeter. Find the dimensions of such a lot. The lots in one area have a stream running along the back of them. Of the lots with the stream at the back, find the dimensions of the lot with the least perimeter. Of the two lots, which takes the *least* amount of fence?

Chapter 5

Group Activity

Find the growth (or decline) of the population of your town in recent years. Write a function which projects this pattern into the future. What will be the projected population in the year 2000? 25 years from now? the year you graduate from college? How valid do you think these projections are? Explain. Does your function model the past also? How close does this function predict the population 10 years ago? 25 years ago? Explain the differences you found, if any.

Student Log (or Journal)

What should you look for in the method a bank uses to calculate the interest on your savings account? Why? What difference does it make to you?

Open-ended Question

Estimate the thickness of a sheet of paper. Then represent mathematically the tearing of a sheet into two pieces, placing them on top of each other, tearing the halves into two pieces each (now you have fourths), stacking them and tearing into two pieces again, and so on. How tall will the stack be after you have torn the paper 10 times? 25 times? 50 times? How many times can you physically still do the tearing?

Chapter 6

Group Activity

Traffic is said to be cyclic (periodic) in nature. Design an experiment in which you collect data about the traffic patterns at a particular spot in your town or near your school. Plot the data and try to find the function that best describes the pattern.

Student Log (or Journal)

How would it be possible to use trigonometry to measure the distance to a star? How can a triangle be formed? What measurements would you know?

Open-ended Question

Two tracking stations s miles apart measure the angle of elevation of a weather balloon to be α and β, respectively (see figure at the top of the next page). Derive a formula for the altitude, h, of the balloon in terms of the angles α and β. Ignore the curvature of Earth.

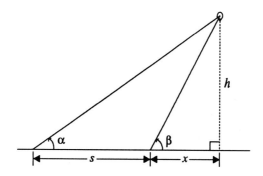

(Problem found in Kastner, B. (1985). *Space Mathematics.* Reston, VA: NCTM.)

Chapter 7

Group Activity
Identify some careers that use trigonometry on a daily basis. (Do not include a mathematics teacher.) Each group member should choose one of these careers and investigate the specific uses of trigonometry. Reports are to be made back to the group and the group will then compile a final report to be delivered to the whole class.

Student Log (or Journal)
Discuss the potential uses of trigonometry in your chosen career. What uses of trigonometry do you think might be hidden in that career, that is, although you may not be doing trigonometry on a daily basis, the work you do relies upon trigonometry in some way.

Open-ended Question
In Section 7.4, it is stated that the graphs of the functions corresponding to a given identity can be used in the verification of that identity but that they are not a verification in and of themselves. The algebra must be done in order to verify the identity. Why is this so?

Chapter 8

Group Activity
Draw a diagram representing the orbit of a satellite above Earth. If such an orbit is 1600 km above the surface of the planet, what other information would be needed to predict when the satellite would be directly overhead? Find the needed information. Create a problem for one of the other groups to solve based upon the data you researched.

Student Log (or Journal)
Imagine a time when we will be able to travel to other words. What laws of physics do you think will remain constant? Which laws do you think will be different in space or on other planets? What changes in our lives could result from these differences?

Open-ended Question
Represent your route from your home to school using vectors. Be ready to explain all parts of your vector map.

Chapter 9

Group Activity
Investigate the polar graphs of $y = \cos \frac{n}{k}x$ and $y = \sin \frac{n}{k}x$, where n and k are integers. Make conjectures that connect the values of n, k, and the graph of the equation. Pay particular attention to the odd/even nature of n and k.

Student Log (or Journal)
Use Definition 9.7 to construct a parabola, ellipse, and hyperbola.

Open-ended Question
Mars travels in an elliptical orbit about the sun. Its shortest distance from the sun (its perihelion) is 129 million miles and its greatest distance (its aphelion) is 154 million miles. Determine the equation of its orbit. Hint: Place the sun at the origin.

Chapter 10

Group Activity
Find the characteristic polynomial, $C(x)$, for the matrix $A = \begin{pmatrix} 2 & 7 & 5 \\ -2 & 8 & 6 \\ 2 & -4 & 8 \end{pmatrix}$. (See Exercise 38 in Section 10.3). Graph $C(x)$ to find the eigenvalues of A.

Student Log (or Journal)
Describe the usefulness of the graphing calculator in the simultaneous solution of a system of equations. How do the graphs help you in solving these types of problems?

Open-ended Question
Find the inverse of the matrix $A = \begin{pmatrix} 2 & 7 & 5 \\ -2 & 8 & 6 \\ 2 & -4 & 8 \end{pmatrix}$. Justify that it is indeed the inverse of A.

Chapter 11

Group Activity
Find the area under the curve $y = \sqrt{49 - x^2}$ and above the x-axis. You may want to graph the function on paper as well as on a graphing calculator. Try dividing the region into vertical rectangles of equal bases with one of the upper corners on the curve. Be ready to explain your methods to the rest of the class.

Student Log (or Journal)
Describe the similarities and differences between *sequences, series,* and *sequences of partial sums.*

Open-ended Question
Draw a square with sides of length 2 units. Connect the midpoints of adjacent sides of the square to form an *interior* square. Repeat the process to make a total of five interior squares. Write the sequence of numbers that represents the areas of the first five interior squares. What rule can be used to find the area of the nth interior square?

Chapter 12

Group Activity
Design an experiment that can be conducted in your school, community, or home. Use the measures of central tendency (mean, median, mode, variance, standard deviation) discussed in this chapter to aid the creation of a report about the experiment to the rest of the class.

Student Log (or Journal)
Discuss the difference between experimental probability and theoretical probability. Are they ever the same? What types of influences create the differences?

Open-ended Question
Choose a particular hand in a card game, such as bridge, and find the probability of receiving that hand according to the rules of the game. Be ready to justify your answer.

Chapter 1 Test–Form A

Directions:

Show all work where appropriate. Circle the **best** answer for each multiple-choice question. A graphing calculator may be necessary to answer some questions.

Each problem is worth 6 points. Scores can range from 4 through 100 points.

(1.1) 1.   What is the distance between the points $(-1, 3)$ and $(4, -5)$?

    A. $\sqrt{13}$

    B. $\sqrt{73}$

    C. $\sqrt{89}$

    D.   29

    E.   89

(1.1) 2. $|3 - \sqrt{11}| =$

    A. $\sqrt{3 - 11}$

    B. $\sqrt{11 - 3}$

    C. $3 - \sqrt{11}$

    D. $\sqrt{11} - 3$

    E.   None of the above.

(1.1) 3.   The distance on the real number line between x and -2 is

    A. $|x + 2|$

    B. $|x - 2|$

    C. $x + 2$

    D. $x - 2$

    E.   None of the above.

Questions 4 and 5 refer to the figure below.

Three sides of a fence and an existing wall form a rectangular enclosure. The *total* length of fence used is 240 feet. Let x be the length of the two sides perpendicular to the wall.

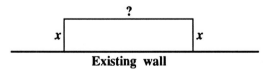

(1.2) 4.   Write the *area A of the enclosure* as a function of the length x of the rectangular area as shown in the above figure.

    A. $A(x) = 240x - 2x^2$

    B. $A(x) = 120x - 2x^2$

    C. $A(x) = 2x + 120$

    D. $A(x) = 240x$

    E. $A(x) = 240 - 2x^2$

(1.2) 5.   The possible values of x that make sense in this problem situation are

    A.   All real numbers.

    B. $x > 0$

    C. $0 < x < 240$

    D. $0 < x < 120$

    E. $x > 240$

(1.2) 6.   Which ONE of the following viewing rectangles gives the best *complete* graph of $y = 30 - 2x + x^2$.

    A. $[-10, 10]$ by $[-10, 10]$

    B. $[-5, 5]$ by $[-15, 15]$

    C. $[0, 10]$ by $[0, 100]$

    D. $[-5, 5]$ by $[-10, 30]$

    E. $[-5, 5]$ by $[0, 50]$

(1.3) 7.   Let $f(x) = \dfrac{1}{x-3}$. Compute $f(2)$.

    A. -1

    B. $-\dfrac{1}{2}$

    C. $-\dfrac{1}{5}$

    D. $\dfrac{1}{5}$

    E. $\dfrac{1}{2}$

(1.3) 8.   Determine the **domain** of the real-valued function $f(x) = \sqrt{x+2}$.

    A. $x > -2$

    B. $x < -2$

    C. $x \geq -2$

    D. $x \leq -2$

    E. $-2 < x < 2$

(1.4) 9.   An equation for the horizontal line through the point $(-1, 2)$ is

    A. $y = -1$

    B. $y = 2$

    C. $x = -1$

    D. $x = 2$

    E.   None of the above.

(1.4) 10.   Write an equation for the line through the point $(-1, 2)$ and perpendicular to the line with equation $2x - 3y - 5 = 0$.

    A. $3x - 2y + 7 = 0$

    B. $x - 2y + 3 = 0$

    C. $3x + 2y - 1 = 0$

    D. $2x + 3y - 4 = 0$

    E. $2x - 3y + 8 = 0$

(1.4) 11.   Assume f is a linear function. If $f(2) = 10$ and $f(0) = 4$, determine a formula for f.

A. $f(x) = \dfrac{1}{3}x + 4$

B. $f(x) = 2x + 10$

C. $f(x) = 3x + 4$

D. $f(x) = 3x + 10$

E. $f(x) = 10x + 4$

(1.5) 12.   The following three transformations are applied (in the given order) to the graph of $y = x^2$:

I.   Vertical stretch by a factor of 3.

II.   Horizontal shift right 2 units.

III. Vertical shift up 4 units.

Which of the following is an equation for the graph produced as a result of applying these transformations?

A. $y = 3(x - 2)^2 + 4$

B. $y = 3(x + 2)^2 + 4$

C. $y = 3(x - 2)^2 - 4$

D. $y = 3(x + 2)^2 - 4$

E.   None of the above.

(1.5) 13.   Assume that the point $(3, 4)$ is on the graph of the function $y = f(x)$. If the point $(2, b)$ is on the graph of $y = f(x + 1)$, then the value of b is

A.   0

B.   1

C.   2

D.   3

E.   None of the above.

(1.5) 14.   A graph of a parabola has line of symmetry $x = 3$ and contains the points $(1, 0)$ and $(3, -4)$. Determine an equation for the parabola.

A. $y = 2(x + 3)^2 - 2$

B. $y = 2(x - 3)^2 - 2$

C. $y = 2(x + 3)^2 - 4$

D. $y = (x - 3)^2 - 4$

E. $y = (x + 3)^2 - 4$

(1.6) 15.   Let $f(x) = x^2 - 2$ and $g(x) = \dfrac{x - 4}{2}$. Compute $f \circ g(6)$.

A.   1

B. -1

C.   15

D.   0

E.   None of the above.

(1.6) 16.   Determine the domain and the range of the function $f(x) = \dfrac{|x-2|}{x-2}$.

    A.   domain of $f = (-\infty, 2) \cup (2, \infty)$, range of $f = \{-1, 1\}$

    B.   domain of $f = (-\infty, -2) \cup (-2, \infty)$, range of $f = \{-1, 1\}$

    C.   domain of $f = (-\infty, 1) \cup (1, \infty)$, range of $f = \{-2, 2\}$

    D.   domain of $f = (-\infty, -1) \cup (-1, \infty)$, range of $f = \{-2, 2\}$

    E.   None of the above.

Chapter 1 Test–Form A
Answer Sheet

1. Answer: A B [C] D E
2. Answer: A B C [D] E
3. Answer: [A] B C D E
4. Answer: [A] B C D E
5. Answer: A B C [D] E
6. Answer: A B C D [E]
7. Answer: [A] B C D E
8. Answer: A B [C] D E
9. Answer: A [B] C D E
10. Answer: A B [C] D E
11. Answer: A B [C] D E
12. Answer: [A] B C D E
13. Answer: A B C D [E]
14. Answer: A B C [D] E
15. Answer: A [B] C D E
16. Answer: [A] B C D E

Chapter 1 Test–Form B

Directions:

Show all work where appropriate. Circle the **best** answer for each multiple-choice question. A graphing calculator may be necessary to answer some questions.

Each problem is worth 6 points. Scores can range from 4 through 100 points.

(1.1) 1. What is the distance between the points $(-1, 2)$ and $(3, -5)$?

     A. $\sqrt{11}$

     B. $\sqrt{53}$

     C. $\sqrt{65}$

     D.   23

     E.   65

(1.1) 2. $|5 - \sqrt{13}| =$

     A. $\sqrt{5 - 13}$

     B. $\sqrt{13 - 5}$

     C. $5 - \sqrt{13}$

     D. $\sqrt{13} - 5$

     E.   None of the above.

(1.1) 3. The distance on the real number line between x and -4 is

     A. $|x + 4|$

     B. $|x - 4|$

     C. $x + 4$

     D. $x - 4$

     E.   None of the above.

Questions 4 and 5 refer to the figure below.

Three sides of a fence and an existing wall form a rectangular enclosure. The *total* length of fence used is 160 feet. Let x be the length of the two sides perpendicular to the wall.

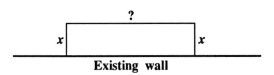

Existing wall

(1.2) 4. Write the *area A of the enclosure* as a function of the length x of the rectangular area as shown in the above figure.

     A. $A(x) = 160 - 2x^2$

     B. $A(x) = 160x$

     C. $A(x) = 2x + 80$

     D. $A(x) = 80x - 2x^2$

     E. $A(x) = 160x - 2x^2$

(1.2) 5.   The possible values of x that make sense in this problem situation are

   A. $x > 0$
   B. $0 < x < 160$
   C. $0 < x < 80$
   D. $x > 160$
   E.   All real numbers.

(1.2) 6.   Which ONE of the following viewing rectangles gives the best *complete* graph of
            $y = 20 - 2x + x^2$.

   A. $[-10, 10]$ by $[-10, 10]$
   B. $[-5, 5]$ by $[-15, 15]$
   C. $[0, 10]$ by $[0, 100]$
   D. $[-5, 5]$ by $[0, 50]$
   E. $[-5, 5]$ by $[-20, 20]$

(1.3) 7.   Let $f(x) = \dfrac{1}{x - 7}$. Compute $f(2)$.

   A. -1
   B. $-\dfrac{1}{2}$
   C. $-\dfrac{1}{5}$
   D. $\dfrac{1}{7}$
   E. $\dfrac{1}{7}$

(1.3) 8.   Determine the **domain** of the real-valued function $f(x) = \sqrt{x + 4}$.

   A. $x \geq -4$
   B. $x \leq -4$
   C. $x \geq 2$
   D. $x \leq 2$
   E. $-2 < x < 2$

(1.4) 9.   An equation for the horizontal line through the point $(2, -1)$ is

   A. $y = -1$
   B. $y = 2$
   C. $x = -1$
   D. $x = 2$
   E.   None of the above.

(1.4) 10.   Write an equation for the line through the point $(-1, 2)$ and perpendicular to the line with
            equation $3x - 2y - 5 = 0$.

   A. $3x - 2y + 7 = 0$
   B. $x - 2y + 3 = 0$
   C. $3x + 2y - 1 = 0$
   D. $2x + 3y - 4 = 0$
   E. $2x - 3y + 8 = 0$

(1.4) 11.   Assume f is a linear function. If $f(2) = 14$ and $f(0) = 10$, determine a formula for f.

    A. $f(x) = \dfrac{1}{3}x + 4$

    B. $f(x) = 2x + 10$

    C. $f(x) = 3x + 4$

    D. $f(x) = 3x + 10$

    E. $f(x) = 10x + 4$

(1.5) 12.   The following three transformations are applied (in the given order) to the graph of $y = x^2$:

    I.   Vertical stretch by a factor of 2.

    II. Horizontal shift left 3 units.

    III. Vertical shift down 4 units.

Which of the following is an equation for the graph produced as a result of applying these transformations?

    A. $y = 2(x - 3)^2 + 4$

    B. $y = 2(x + 3)^2 + 4$

    C. $y = 2(x - 3)^2 - 4$

    D. $y = 2(x + 3)^2 - 4$

    E.   None of the above.

(1.5) 13.   Assume that the point $(2, 3)$ is on the graph of the function $y = f(x)$. If the point $(1, b)$ is on the graph of $y = f(x + 1)$, then the value of b is

    A.   0

    B.   1

    C.   2

    D.   3

    E.   None of the above.

(1.5) 14.   A graph of a parabola has line of symmetry $x = -3$ and contains the points $(-5, 0)$ and $(-3, -4)$. Determine an equation for the parabola.

    A. $y = 2(x + 3)^2 - 2$

    B. $y = 2(x - 3)^2 - 2$

    C. $y = 2(x + 3)^2 - 4$

    D. $y = (x - 3)^2 - 4$

    E. $y = (x + 3)^2 - 4$

(1.6) 15.   Let $f(x) = x^2 - 3$ and $g(x) = \dfrac{x - 4}{2}$. Compute $f \circ g(6)$.

    A.   0

    B.   2

    C. -2

    D.   14.5

    E.   None of the above.

(1.6) 16. Determine the domain and the range of the function $f(x) = \dfrac{|x+3|}{x+3}$.

A. domain of $f = (-\infty, -3) \cup (-3, \infty)$, range of $f = \{-1, 1\}$

B. domain of $f = (-\infty, 3) \cup (3, \infty)$, range of $f = \{-1, 1\}$

C. domain of $f = (-\infty, -1) \cup (-1, \infty)$, range of $f = \{-3, 3\}$

D. domain of $f = (-\infty, 1) \cup (1, \infty)$, range of $f = \{-3, 3\}$

E. None of the above.

Chapter 1 Test–Form B

Answer Sheet

1.   Answer: A B [C] D E

2.   Answer: A B C [D] E

3.   Answer: [A] B C D E

4.   Answer: A B C D [E]

5.   Answer: A B [C] D E

6.   Answer: A B C [D] E

7.   Answer: A B [C] D E

8.   Answer: [A] B C D E

9.   Answer: [A] B C D E

10.   Answer: A B C [D] E

11.   Answer: A [B] C D E

12.   Answer: A B C [D] E

13.   Answer: A B C [D] E

14.   Answer: A B C D [E]

15.   Answer: A B [C] D E

16.   Answer: [A] B C D E

Chapter 2 Test–Form A

Directions:

Show all work where appropriate. Circle the **best** answer for each multiple-choice question. A graphing calculator may be necessary to answer some questions.

Each problem is worth 6 points. Scores can range from 4 through 100 points.

(2.3) 1.   Solve the equation $\frac{1}{4}x - 3 = 5x$.

A. $x = \frac{4}{7}$

B. $x = \frac{19}{12}$

C. $x = -\frac{19}{12}$

D. $x = \frac{12}{19}$

E. $x = -\frac{12}{19}$

(2.3) 2.   Solve the equation $x^2 - 3x - 7 = 0$.

A. $x = \frac{-3 \pm \sqrt{37}}{2}$

B. $x = -3 \pm \frac{\sqrt{37}}{2}$

C. $x = \frac{3 \pm \sqrt{37}}{2}$

D. $x = 3 \pm \frac{\sqrt{37}}{2}$

E.   There are no real solutions.

(2.4) 3.   Solve the inequality $-2x - 4 > 6$.

A. $x < -5$

B. $x > -5$

C. $x < -1$

D. $x > -1$

E.   None of the above.

(2.4) 4.   Choose the inequality that is equivalent to $5 - 2x \geq \frac{3x - 1}{2}$.

A. $x \leq \frac{11}{7}$

B. $x \geq \frac{11}{7}$

C. $x \leq -\frac{11}{7}$

D. $x \leq \frac{11}{5}$

E. $x \geq \frac{11}{5}$

(2.4) 5.   Solve $|x - 4| > 8$.

    A. $(12, \infty)$

    B. $(-4, 12)$

    C. $(-\infty, -4) \cup (12, \infty)$

    D. $(-\infty, -12) \cup (4, \infty)$

    E. $(12, -4)$

(2.5) 6.   Solve for x : $3x^2 - 5x < 2$.

    A. $x > 2$ or $x < -\dfrac{1}{3}$

    B. $-\dfrac{1}{3} < x < 2$

    C. $x > \dfrac{1}{3}$ or $x < -2$

    D. $-2 < x < \dfrac{1}{3}$

    E. $-\dfrac{2}{3} < x < 1$

Questions 7 through 9 refer to the following:

The length of a rectangle is 7 units more than its width.

(2.2) 7.   Let x be the width of the rectangle. Write the length L as a function.

    A. $L = 7 - x$

    B. $L = x - 7$

    C. $L = x + 7$

    D. $L = 7x$

    E.   None of the above.

(2.2) 8.   Write the area of the rectangle as a function of x .

    A. $A = x(7 - x)$

    B. $A = x(x - 7)$

    C. $A = x(x + 7)$

    D. $A = 7x^2$

    E.   None of the above.

(2.2) 9.   Find the **length** of the rectangle if its area is 60 square units.

    A.   3

    B.   6

    C.   10

    D.   12

    E.   15

(2.1) 10.   Use a graphing utility to determine the *number* of real solutions to the equation $4x^3 - 10x + 17 = 0$.

A.   0

B.   1

C.   2

D.   3

E.   4

(2.1) 11.   Use a graphing utility to find *one* real solution to the equation $4x^3 - 4x^2 + x - 2 = 0$. Determine your answer with error of at most 0.01.

(2.5) 12.   Use a graphing utility to estimate the solution to the inequality $x^3 - 5x + 8 \geq 25$. State the viewing rectangle used to obtain your estimate.

Questions 13 and 14 refer to the figure below.

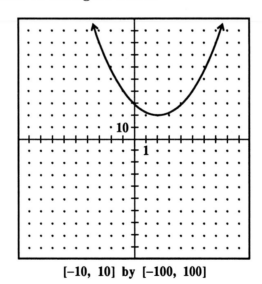

[−10, 10] by [−100, 100]

(2.6) 13.   Fill in the following table.

x	y
−1	
0	
2	
	70
	10

(2.6) 14.   Is the relation given by the graph a function? _____ (yes or no)

(2.7) 15. Which of the following functions have inverses that are functions?

$$f(x) = -\frac{1}{2}x - 3, \quad h(x) = \frac{1}{x-3}, \quad k(x) = x^3 - x$$

A. f, h, and k

B. h and k only

C. f only

D. f and h only

E. None of the above.

(2.7) 16. Let $f(x) = \sqrt{x+3}$.

(a) Why does f have an inverse that is a function?

(b) Find a rule for $f^{-1}(x)$.

Chapter 2 Test–Form A

Answer Sheet

1.   Answer: A   B   C   D $\boxed{\text{E}}$

2.   Answer: A   B $\boxed{\text{C}}$ D   E

3.   Answer: $\boxed{\text{A}}$ B   C   D   E

4.   Answer: $\boxed{\text{A}}$ B   C   D   E

5.   Answer: A   B $\boxed{\text{C}}$ D   E

6.   Answer: A $\boxed{\text{B}}$ C   D   E

7.   Answer: A   B $\boxed{\text{C}}$ D   E

8.   Answer: A   B $\boxed{\text{C}}$ D   E

9.   Answer: A   B   C $\boxed{\text{D}}$ E

10. Answer: A $\boxed{\text{B}}$ C   D   E

11. Answer: $x \approx 1.16$

12. Answer: $x \geq 3.20$
     Viewing Rectangle: Answers will vary.

13.

x	y
-1	40
0	30
2	20
$-2.65, 6.5$	70
none	10

14. Answer: yes

15. Answer: A   B   C $\boxed{\text{D}}$ E

16. a) f is one-to-one.

     b) $y = x^2 - 3$ for $x \geq 0$

Chapter 2 Test–Form B

Directions:

Show all work where appropriate. Circle the **best** answer for each multiple-choice question. A graphing calculator may be necessary to answer some questions.

Each problem is worth 6 points. Scores can range from 4 through 100 points.

(2.3) 1. Solve the equation $\frac{1}{5}x - 3 = 4x$.

A. $x = -1$

B. $x = -5$

C. $x = -\frac{3}{19}$

D. $x = -\frac{15}{19}$

E. $x = \frac{3}{19}$

(2.3) 2. Solve the equation $x^2 - 7x - 3 = 0$.

A. $x = \frac{-7 \pm \sqrt{61}}{2}$

B. $x = \frac{7 \pm \sqrt{61}}{2}$

C. $x = -7 \pm \frac{\sqrt{61}}{2}$

D. $x = 7 \pm \frac{\sqrt{61}}{2}$

E. There are no real solutions.

(2.4) 3. Solve the inequality $-2x - 6 > 8$.

A. $x < -1$

B. $x > -1$

C. $x < -7$

D. $x > -7$

E. None of the above.

(2.4) 4. Choose the inequality that is equivalent to $5 - 2x \geq \frac{2x - 1}{3}$.

A. $x \leq \frac{3}{4}$

B. $x \geq \frac{3}{4}$

C. $x \geq 4$

D. $x \leq 4$

E. $x \leq 2$

(2.4) 5.   Solve $|x - 8| > 4$.

   A. $(12, \infty)$
   B. $(-4, 12)$
   C. $(-\infty, -4) \cup (4, \infty)$
   D. $(-\infty, 4) \cup (12, \infty)$
   E. $(-\infty, -4) \cup (12, \infty)$

(2.5) 6.   Solve for x: $3x^2 - 5x > 2$.

   A. $x > 2$ or $x < -\dfrac{1}{3}$

   B. $-\dfrac{1}{3} < x < 2$

   C. $x > \dfrac{1}{3}$ or $x < -2$

   D. $-2 < x < \dfrac{1}{3}$

   E. $-\dfrac{2}{3} < x < 1$

Questions 7 through 9 refer to the following:

   The length of a rectangle is 9 units more than its width.

(2.2) 7.   Let x be the width of the rectangle. Write the length L as a function.

   A. $L = 9x$
   B. $L = x + 9$
   C. $L = x - 9$
   D. $L = 9 - x$
   E.   None of the above.

(2.2) 8.   Write the area of the rectangle as a function of x.

   A. $A = 9x^2$
   B. $A = x(x + 9)$
   C. $A = x(x - 9)$
   D. $A = x(9 - x)$
   E.   None of the above.

(2.2) 9.   Find the **length** of the rectangle if its area is 70 square units.

   A.   2
   B.   7
   C.   10
   D.   14
   E.   35

(2.1) 10.   Use a graphing utility to determine the *number* of real solutions to the equation
$4x^3 - 10x + 5 = 0$.

    A.   0

    B.   1

    C.   2

    D.   3

    E.   4

(2.1) 11.   Use a graphing utility to find *one* real solution to the equation $4x^3 - 4x^2 + x - 3 = 0$.
Determine your answer with error of at most 0.01.

(2.5) 12.   Use a graphing utility to estimate the solution to the inequality $x^3 - 7x + 9 \geq 25$. State the
viewing rectangle used to obtain your estimate.

Questions 13 and 14 refer to the figure below.

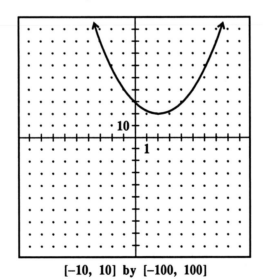

[−10, 10] by [−100, 100]

(2.6) 13.   Fill in the following table.

x	y
−1	
0	
2	
	70
	10

(2.6) 14.   Is the relation given by the graph a function? _____ (yes or no)

(2.7) 15.   Which of the following functions have inverses that are functions?

$$f(x) = 3x + 4, \quad h(x) = \frac{1}{x + 2}, \quad k(x) = x^3 + x$$

A. f, h, and k

B. h and k only

C. f only

D. f and h only

E.   None of the above.

(2.7) 16.   Let $f(x) = \sqrt{x - 2}$.

(a)   Why does f have an inverse that is a function?

(b)   Find a rule for $f^{-1}(x)$.

Chapter 2 Test–Form B

Answer Sheet

1.   Answer: A   B   C $\boxed{\text{D}}$ E

2.   Answer: A $\boxed{\text{B}}$ C   D   E

3.   Answer: A   B $\boxed{\text{C}}$ D   E

4.   Answer: A   B   C   D $\boxed{\text{E}}$

5.   Answer: A   B   C $\boxed{\text{D}}$ E

6.   Answer: $\boxed{\text{A}}$ B   C   D   E

7.   Answer: A $\boxed{\text{B}}$ C   D   E

8.   Answer: A $\boxed{\text{B}}$ C   D   E

9.   Answer: A   B   C $\boxed{\text{D}}$ E

10.   Answer: A   B   C $\boxed{\text{D}}$ E

11.   Answer: 1.27

12.   Answer: $x \geq 3.42$
      Viewing Rectangle: Answers will vary.

13.

x	y
−1	**5**
0	**40**
2	**30**
2, 6	70
none	10

14.   Answer: yes

15.   Answer: $\boxed{\text{A}}$ B   C   D   E

16.   a) f is one-to-one.

      b) $y = x^2 + 2$, for $x \geq 0$

Chapter 3 Test–Form A

Directions:

Show all work where appropriate. Circle the **best** answer for each multiple-choice question. A graphing calculator may be necessary to answer some questions.

Each problem is worth 6 points. Scores can range from 4 through 100 points.

(3.2) 1.   Which of the functions is an **end behavior model** of $f(x) = 2 - 2x + 3x^2 - 4x^3$.

    A. x^3

    B. $-x^3$

    C. $4x^3$

    D. $-4x^3$

    E.   None of the above.

(3.2) 2.   Which statement best describes the end behavior of $f(x) = 3x^4 - 2x^3 + 3x - 5$?

    A. $f(x) \to -\infty$ as $x \to \infty$ and $f(x) \to \infty$ as $x \to -\infty$

    B. $f(x) \to \infty$ as $|x| \to \infty$

    C. $f(x) \to -\infty$ as $|x| \to \infty$

    D. $f(x) \to \infty$ as $x \to \infty$ and $f(x) \to -\infty$ as $x \to -\infty$

    E.   None of the above.

(3.6) 3.   Which one of the following could represent a complete graph of $f(x) = x^3 + ax$ where a is a real number?

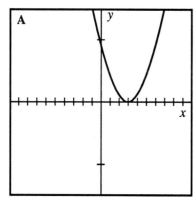 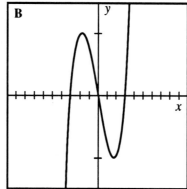 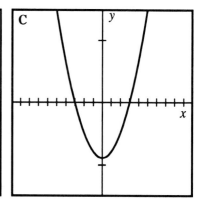

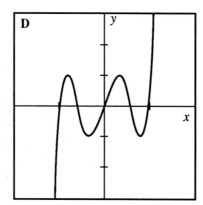 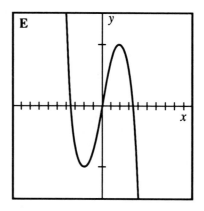

(3.5) 4.   Which of the following is a zero of $f(x) = x^3 + 2x^2 - 3$?

A. $\dfrac{3}{2} + \dfrac{\sqrt{3}}{2}i$

B. $\dfrac{3}{2} - \dfrac{\sqrt{3}}{2}i$

C. $-\dfrac{3}{2} + \dfrac{\sqrt{3}}{2}i$

D. $-3 - \dfrac{\sqrt{3}}{2}i$

E. $-3 + \dfrac{\sqrt{3}}{2}i$

(3.3) 5.   Divide $x^3 - 2x^2 + 3x - 2$ by $x - 3$. The quotient polynomial is

A. $x^2 + x + 6$

B. $x^2 - x - 6$

C. $x^2 - 5x + 18$

D. $x^2 + 5x - 18$

E. $x^2 - 5x - 18$

(3.3) 6.   What is the remainder when $x^{32} - 5x^{15} + 12$ is divided by $x + 1$?

A.   0

B.   6

C.   8

D.   16

E.   18

Problems 7 through 9 refer to the polynomial $f(x) = 2x^3 + 2x^2 - 5x - 5$.

(3.4) 7.   Use the Rational Roots Theorem to list **all** the possible candidates for rational roots of the polynomial $f(x)$.

A.   1 , 2 , ± 5

B. ± 1 , ± 2 , $\pm\dfrac{1}{5}$, $\pm\dfrac{2}{5}$

C. ± 1 , $\pm\dfrac{1}{2}$, ± 5 , $\pm\dfrac{5}{2}$

D. ± 1 , ± 2 , ± 5 , $\pm\dfrac{2}{5}$

E. ± 1 , ± 2 , ± 5

(3.4) 8.   Use a graph to eliminate some or all of the possibilities from the list in Question 7 above. List the remaining candidates for the **rational** roots of $f(x)$.

(3.4) 9.   Determine the **real** zeros of $f(x)$.

(3.1) 10.   Use a graphing utility to **estimate all** local maximum and minimum values of
             $f(x) = 2x^4 - 17x^3 + 37x^2 - 7x - 15$.

    A. $-\dfrac{1}{2}$, 1, 3, 5

    B. -29, -15, 15

    C. -15, 15, 29

    D. -29, 15

    E.   The function f does not have a local maximum or minimum.

(3.1) 11.   Determine the **range** of $f(x) = 3 - 20x - x^2 - 3x^4$. The answers listed are approximations.

    A. $y \geq 0$

    B. $y \geq 20$

    C. $y \leq 20$

    D. $y \geq 3$

    E. $y \leq 3$

(3.5) 12.   Which one of the following is a polynomial with **real** coefficients that has -2 and $2 + i$ as
             zeros?

    A. $(x + 2)(x - 2 - i)$

    B. $(x - 2)(x + 2 + i)$

    C. $(x + 2)(x^2 - 4x + 5)$

    D. $(x - 2)(x^2 - 4x + 5)$

    E. $(x + 2)(x^2 + 5)$

(3.2) 13.   The figure below shows a rectangle with its base on the x-axis and its upper two vertices on
             the graph of the equation $y = 9 - x^2$.

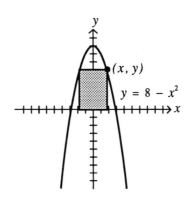

    Which of the following represents the **area** of this rectangle as a function of x.

    A. $f(x) = 9 - x^2$

    B. $f(x) = 9x - x^3$

    C. $f(x) = 18 - 2x^2$

    D. $f(x) = 18x - 2x^3$

    E.   None of the above.

(3.1) 14.   Which one of the following could represent a complete graph of $f(x) = -x^4 + x^3 + px^2 + qx + r$, where p, q, and r are real numbers?

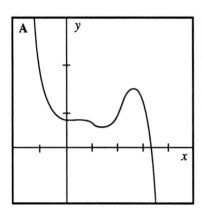

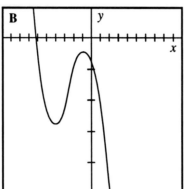

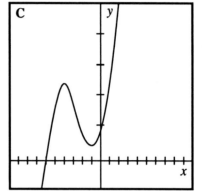

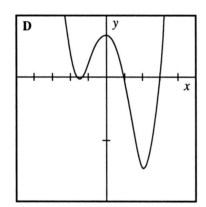

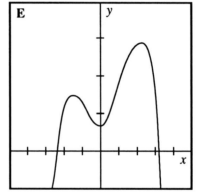

Problems 15 and 16 refer to the following system:

$$y = 4 - x^2 + 3x^3$$
$$y = -1 + 2x$$

(3.7) 15.   Use a graphing utility to determine the *number* of solutions to the above system.

    A.   0
    B.   1
    C.   2
    D.   3
    E.   4

(3.7) 16.   Use a graphing utility to find *one* solution to the above system. Determine your answer with error of at most 0.01.

Chapter 3 Test–Form A

Answer Sheet

1. Answer: A B C [D] E

2. Answer: A [B] C D E

3. Answer: A [B] C D E

4. Answer: A B [C] D E

5. Answer: [A] B C D E

6. Answer: A B C D [E]

7. Answer: A B [C] D E

8. Answer: -1

9. Answer: $\pm\sqrt{\dfrac{5}{2}}$ and -1

10. Answer: A [B] C D E

11. Answer: A B [C] D E

12. Answer: A B [C] D E

13. Answer: A B C [D] E

14. Answer: A B C D [E]

15. Answer: A [B] C D E

16. Answer: (x, y) such that $x \in [-1.26, -1.24]$ and $y \in [-3.52, -3.5]$

Chapter 3 Test–Form B

Directions:

Show all work where appropriate. Circle the **best** answer for each multiple-choice question. A graphing calculator may be necessary to answer some questions.

Each problem is worth 6 points. Scores can range from 4 through 100 points.

(3.2) 1.   Which of the functions is an **end behavior model** of $f(x) = 2 - 2x + 3x^2 - x^3$.

    A. x^3

    B. $-x^3$

    C. $4x^3$

    D. $-4x^3$

    E.   None of the above.

(3.2) 2.   Which statement best describes the end behavior of $f(x) = -2x^4 - 3x^3 + 3x - 5$?

    A. $f(x) \to -\infty$ as $x \to \infty$ and $f(x) \to \infty$ as $x \to -\infty$

    B. $f(x) \to \infty$ as $|x| \to \infty$

    C. $f(x) \to -\infty$ as $|x| \to \infty$

    D. $f(x) \to \infty$ as $x \to \infty$ and $f(x) \to -\infty$ as $x \to -\infty$

    E.   None of the above.

(3.6) 3.   Which one of the following could represent a complete graph of $f(x) = ax - x^3$ where a is a real number?

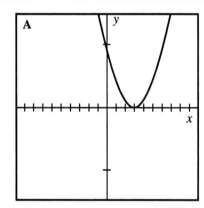
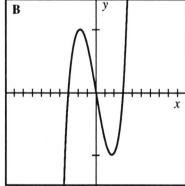
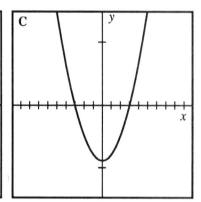

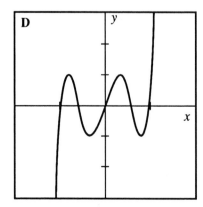
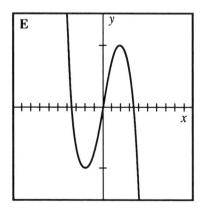

(3.5) 4.   Which of the following is a zero of $f(x) = 2x^3 + x^2 - 3$?

      A. $-\dfrac{3}{4} + \dfrac{\sqrt{15}}{4}i$

      B. $\dfrac{3}{4} - \dfrac{\sqrt{15}}{4}i$

      C. $-\dfrac{3}{4} + \dfrac{\sqrt{15}}{4}i$

      D. $3 + \dfrac{\sqrt{15}}{4}i$

      E. $-3 + \dfrac{\sqrt{15}}{4}i$

(3.3) 5.   Divide $x^3 - 2x^2 + 4x - 2$ by $x - 3$. The quotient polynomial is

      A. $x^2 - x + 1$

      B. $x^2 + x + 7$

      C. $x^2 - 5x + 19$

      D. $x^2 + 5x - 19$

      E. $x^2 + 5x - 19$

(3.3) 6.   What is the remainder when $x^{29} - 7x^{14} + 8$ is divided by $x - 1$?

      A.   0

      B.   2

      C.   14

      D.   16

      E.   23

Questions 7 through 9 refer to the polynomial $f(x) = 5x^3 + 2x^2 - 5x - 2$.

(3.4) 7.   Use the Rational Roots Theorem to list **all** the possible candidates for rational roots of the polynomial $f(x)$.

      A. 1, 2, ± 5

      B. ± 1, ± 2, $\pm\dfrac{1}{5}$, $\pm\dfrac{2}{5}$

      C. ± 1, $\pm\dfrac{1}{2}$, ± 5, $\pm\dfrac{5}{2}$

      D. ± 1, ± 2, ± 5, $\pm\dfrac{2}{5}$

      E. ± 1, ± 2, ± 5

(3.4) 8.   Use a graph to eliminate some or all of the possibilities from the list in Question 7 above. List the remaining candidates for the **rational** roots of $f(x)$.

(3.4) 9   Determine the **real** zeros of $f(x)$.

(3.1) 10.   Use a graphing utility to **estimate all** local maximum and minimum values of
$f(x) = 2x^4 - 17x^3 + 37x^2 - 7x - 10$.

A.   0, 2, 4

B. -24, -10, 20

C. -10, 20, 24

D. -10, 20

E.   The function f does not have a local maximum or minimum.

(3.1) 11.   Determine the **range** of $f(x) = 13 - 20x - x^2 - 3x^4$. The answers listed are approximations.

A. $y \geq 10$

B. $y \geq 30$

C. $y \leq 30$

D. $y \geq 13$

E. $y \leq 13$

(3.5) 12.   Which one of the following is a polynomial with **real** coefficients that has 2 and $2 - i$ as zeros?

A. $(x + 2)(x - 2 - i)$

B. $(x - 2)(x + 2 + i)$

C. $(x + 2)(x^2 - 4x + 5)$

D. $(x - 2)(x^2 - 4x + 5)$

E. $(x + 2)(x^2 + 5)$

(3.2) 13.   The figure below shows a rectangle with its base on the x-axis and its upper two vertices on the graph of the equation $y = 8 - x^2$.

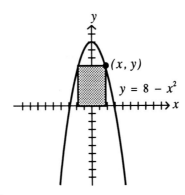

Which of the following represents the **area** of this rectangle as a function of x.

A. $f(x) = 16x - 2x^3$

B. $f(x) = 16 - 2x^2$

C. $f(x) = 8x - x^3$

D. $f(x) = 8 - x^2$

E.   None of the above.

(3.1) 14. Which one of the following could represent a complete graph of $f(x) = x^4 - x^3 + px^2 + qx + r$, where p, q, and r are real numbers?

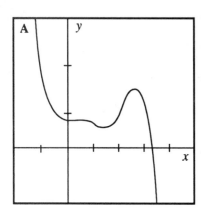

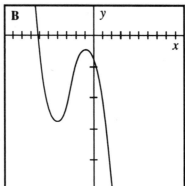

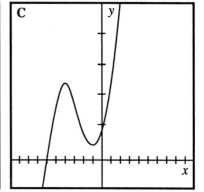

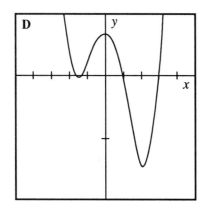

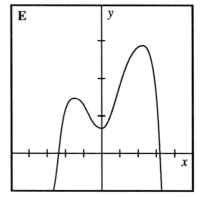

Problems 15 and 16 refer to the following system:

$$y = -1 + 3x^2 + 2x^3$$
$$y = 1 + 4x$$

(3.7) 15. Use a graphing utility to determine the *number* of solutions to the above system.

    A.   0
    B.   1
    C.   2
    D.   3
    E.   4

(3.7) 16. Use a graphing utility to find *one* solution to the above system. Determine your answer with error of at most 0.01.

Chapter 3 Test–Form B

Answer Sheet

1.   Answer: A $\boxed{\text{B}}$ C D E

2.   Answer: A B $\boxed{\text{C}}$ D E

3.   Answer: A B C D $\boxed{\text{E}}$

4.   Answer: $\boxed{\text{A}}$ B C D E

5.   Answer: A $\boxed{\text{B}}$ C D E

6.   Answer: A $\boxed{\text{B}}$ C D E

7.   Answer: A $\boxed{\text{B}}$ C D E

8.   Answer: ± 1, $\pm\dfrac{1}{5}$, $\pm\dfrac{2}{5}$

9.   Answer: -1, $-\dfrac{1}{5}$, $\dfrac{2}{5}$

10.   Answer: A $\boxed{\text{B}}$ C D E

11.   Answer: A B $\boxed{\text{C}}$ D E

12.   Answer: A B C $\boxed{\text{D}}$ E

13.   Answer: $\boxed{\text{A}}$ B C D E

14.   Answer: A B C $\boxed{\text{D}}$ E

15.   Answer: A B C $\boxed{\text{D}}$ E

16.   Answer: -2.20 or -0.41 or 1.11

Chapter 4 Test–Form A

Directions:

Show all work where appropriate. Circle the **best** answer for each multiple-choice question. A graphing calculator may be necessary to answer some questions.

Each problem is worth 6 points. Scores can range from 4 through 100 points.

(4.1) 1.   Let $f(x) = \dfrac{x^2 - 4}{x^2 - 9}$. The *vertical* asymptotes of f are

A. $x = 2$ and $x = -2$.

B. $y = 2$ and $y = -2$.

C. $x = 3$ and $x = -3$.

D. $y = 3$ and $y = -3$.

E.   There are no vertical asymptotes.

(4.4) 2.   Explain how the graph of $y = \sqrt{x - 2}$ can be obtained from the graph of $y = \sqrt{x}$.

(4.4) 3.   The graph of $y = -3 + \dfrac{2}{x-4}$ can be obtained from the graph of $y = \dfrac{1}{x}$ by applying, in order, the following three transformations.

I.   vertical stretch by a factor of a
II.   horizontal shift of b units left or right
III.   vertical shift of c units up or down

What are the values of a, b, and c?

A. $a = 4$, $b = 3$ left, $c = 2$ up

B. $a = 3$, $b = 2$ right, $c = 4$ up

C. $a = 2$, $b = 4$ right, $c = 3$ down

D. $a = 2$, $b = 4$ right, $c = 3$ up

E. $a = 2$, $b = 4$ left, $c = 3$ down

(4.4) 4.   Solve $\sqrt{x - 2} = 8$ for x.

A.   0

B.   10

C. $2\sqrt{2}$

D.   66

E.   There are no real solutions.

(4.1) 5.   Let $g(x) = 2 + \dfrac{1}{x}$. A *horizontal* asymptote of g is

    A. $y = 2$

    B. $y = 0$

    C. $x = 0$

    D. $x = 2$

    E.   There are no horizontal asymptotes.

(4.1) 6.   The *domain* of $f(x) = \dfrac{x + 2}{x^2 + x - 6}$ is

    A. $(-\infty, 3) \cup (3, \infty)$

    B. $(-\infty, 2) \cup (2, \infty)$

    C. $(-\infty, -3) \cup (-3, \infty)$

    D. $(-\infty, -2) \cup (-2, \infty)$

    E.   None of the above.

(4.4) 7.   Sketch a complete graph of $y = -1 + 2\sqrt{x + 4}$. Do not use a graphing utility.

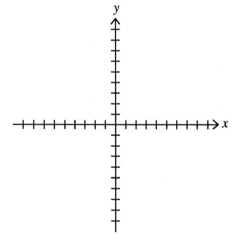

(4.3) 8.   Solve **algebraically** $\dfrac{2x}{x + 4} + \dfrac{3}{x + 1} = \dfrac{24}{(x + 4)(x + 1)}$. Show all steps.

(4.2) 9.　　Sketch a complete graph of $f(x) = x + 4 - \dfrac{1}{x+2}$. Do not use a graphing utility.

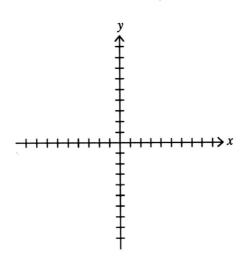

(4.2) 10.　　The end behavior of $f(x) = \dfrac{2x^3 - x + 6}{x + 3}$ is given by

　　A.　　$y = 2x^2 - 7$

　　B.　　$y = 2x^2 - 7x + 21$

　　C.　　$y = 2x^2 - 6x + 17$

　　D.　　$y = 2x^2 + 5x - 15$

　　E.　　$y = 2x^2 + 5$

Questions 11 through 14 refer to the rational function of $f(x) = \dfrac{x^5 - 2x^2 + 4}{x^3 + 8}$.

(4.3) 11.　　All real solutions to $f(x) = 0$ are in the interval

　　A.　　$(-3, -2)$

　　B.　　$(-2, -1)$

　　C.　　$(-1, 0)$

　　D.　　$(0, 1)$

　　E.　　$(1, 2)$

(4.1) 12.　　What happens to the values of $f(x)$ as $x \to -2^+$?

　　A.　　The $f(x)$ values are not real numbers.

　　B.　　$f(x) \to 0$

　　C.　　$f(x) \to -\infty$

　　D.　　$f(x) \to \infty$

　　E.　　$f(x) \to 1$

(4.3) 13. How many local *minimum* values does the function f have?

A.   0

B.   1

C.   2

D.   3

E.   4

(4.2) 14. Sketch a complete graph of f using the information obtained in problems 11–13.

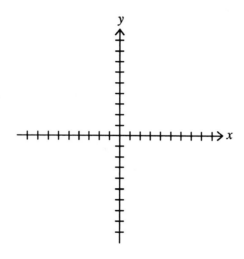

In problems 15 - 16, pure acid is added to 100 ounces of a 56% acid solution. Let x be the amount (in ounces) of pure acid added.

(4.1) 15. Express the concentration C of acid of the mixture as a function of x.

A. $C(x) = \dfrac{56 + x}{x + 100}$

B. $C(x) = \dfrac{56x}{x + 100}$

C. $C(x) = \dfrac{100 + x}{x + 56}$

D. $C(x) = \dfrac{x + 100}{56x}$

A.   None of the above.

(4.1) 16. Determine how much pure acid should be added to the 56% solution to produce a new mixture that is at least 75% acid.

A.   65 ounces

B.   68 ounces

C.   72 ounces

D.   76 ounces

E.   None of the above.

Chapter 4 Test–Form A

Answer Sheet

1. Answer: A B [C] D E

2. Answer: A horizontal shift right of 2 units.

3. Answer: A B [C] D E

4. Answer: A B C [D] E

5. Answer: [A] B C D E

6. Answer: A B C D [E]

7.

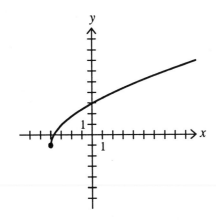

8. Answer: $x = 1.5$

9.

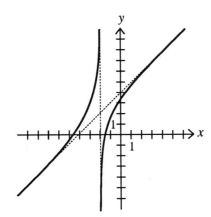

10. Answer: A B [C] D E

11. Answer: A [B] C D E

12. Answer: A B [C] D E

13. Answer: A B [C] D E

14.

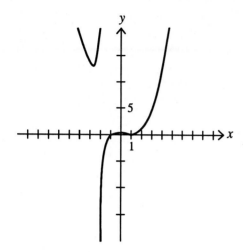

15.   Answer: [A] B C D E

16.   Answer: A B C [D] E

2

Chapter 4 Test–Form B

Directions:

Show all work where appropriate. Circle the **best** answer for each multiple-choice question. A graphing calculator may be necessary to answer some questions.

Each problem is worth 6 points. Scores can range from 4 through 100 points.

(4.1) 1. Let $f(x) = \dfrac{x^2 - 9}{x^2 - 4}$. The *vertical* asymptotes of f are

    A. $x = 2$ and $x = -2$.

    B. $y = 2$ and $y = -2$.

    C. $x = 3$ and $x = -3$.

    D. $y = 3$ and $y = -3$.

    E.   There are no vertical asymptotes.

(4.4) 2. Explain how the graph of $y = \sqrt{x + 3}$ can be obtained from the graph of $y = \sqrt{x}$.

(4.1) 3. The graph of $y = -3 + \dfrac{4}{x+2}$ can be obtained from the graph of $y = \dfrac{1}{x}$ by applying, in order, the following three transformations.

    I.   vertical stretch by a factor of a
    II.   horizontal shift of b units left or right
    III. vertical shift of c units up or down

What are the values of a, b, and c?

    A. $a = 2$, $b = 3$ left, $c = 4$ up

    B. $a = 3$, $b = 2$ right, $c = 4$ up

    C. $a = 4$, $b = 2$ right, $c = 3$ down

    D. $a = 4$, $b = 2$ right, $c = 3$ up

    E. $a = 4$, $b = 2$ left, $c = 3$ down

(4.4) 4. Solve $\sqrt{x - 4} = 8$ for x.

    A.   0

    B.   12

    C. $2\sqrt{2}$

    D.   68

    E.   There are no real solutions.

(4.1) 5.   Let $g(x) = 3 + \dfrac{1}{x}$. A *horizontal* asymptote of g is

A. $x = 3$

B. $x = 0$

C. $y = 0$

D. $y = 3$

E.   There are no horizontal asymptotes.

(4.1) 6.   The *domain* of $f(x) = \dfrac{x-3}{x^2-4}$ is

A. $(-\infty, 3) \cup (3, \infty)$

B. $(-\infty, 2) \cup (2, \infty)$

C. $(-\infty, -3) \cup (-3, \infty)$

D. $(-\infty, -2) \cup (-2, \infty)$

E.   None of the above.

(4.4) 7.   Sketch a complete graph of $y = 3 - \sqrt{x-2}$. Do not use a graphing utility.

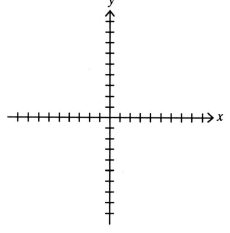

(4.3) 8.   Solve **algebraically** $\dfrac{2x}{x-2} + \dfrac{3}{x+1} = \dfrac{6}{(x-2)(x+1)}$. Show all steps.

(4.2) 9.   Sketch a complete graph of $f(x) = 2x - 3 - \dfrac{1}{x+1}$. Do not use a graphing utility.

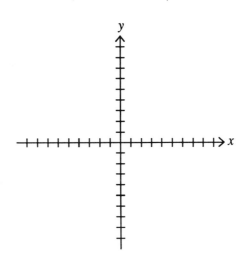

(4.2) 10.   The end behavior of $f(x) = \dfrac{2x^3 - x + 6}{x + 2}$ is given by

    A. $y = 2x^2 - 7$

    B. $y = 2x^2 - 1$

    C. $y = 2x^2 + 4x + 7$

    D. $y = 2x^2 - 4x + 7$

    E. $y = 2x^2 - 4x - 7$

Questions 11 through 14 refer to the rational function $f(x) = \dfrac{x^5 - 2x^2 + 4}{x^3 - 8}$.

(4.3) 11.   All real solutions to $f(x) = 0$ are in the interval

    A. $(-3, -2)$

    B. $(-2, -1)$

    C. $(-1, 0)$

    D. $(0, 1)$

    E. $(1, 2)$

(4.1) 12.   What happens to the values of $f(x)$ as $x \to 2^-$?

    A.   The $f(x)$ values are not real numbers.

    B. $f(x) \to 0$

    C. $f(x) \to -\infty$

    D. $f(x) \to \infty$

    E. $f(x) \to 1$

(4.3) 13. How many local *minimum* values does the function f have?

    A.   0

    B.   1

    C.   2

    D.   3

    E.   4

(4.2) 14. Sketch a complete graph of f using the information obtained in problems 11–13.

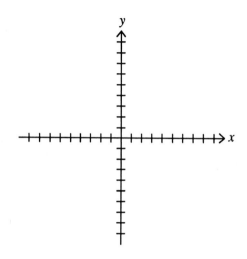

In problems 15 - 16, pure acid is added to 100 grams of a 22% acid solution. Let x be the amount (in grams) of pure acid added.

(4.1) 15. Express the concentration C of acid of the mixture as a function of x.

    A. $C(x) = \dfrac{22 + x}{x + 100}$

    B. $C(x) = \dfrac{22x}{x + 100}$

    C. $C(x) = \dfrac{100 + x}{x + 22}$

    D. $C(x) = \dfrac{x + 100}{22x}$

    A.   None of the above.

(4.1) 16. Determine how much pure acid should be added to the 22% solution to produce a new mixture that is at least 30% acid.

    A.   11.4 grams

    B.   10.4 grams

    C.   9.4 gramss

    D.   8.4 grams

    E.   None of the above.

Chapter 4 Test–Form B

Answer Sheet

1.   Answer: A   B   C   D   E

2.   Answer: horizontal shift left 3 units

3.   Answer: A   B   C   D   E

4.   Answer: A   B   C   D   E

5.   Answer: A   B   C   D   E

6.   Answer: A   B   C   D   E

7.

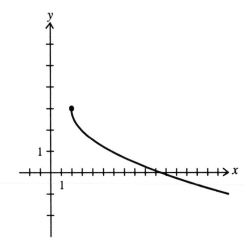

8.   Answer: $x = -4, \dfrac{3}{2}$

9.

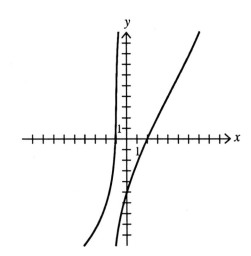

10.   Answer: A   B   C   D   E

11.   Answer: A   B   C   D   E

12.   Answer: A   B   C   D   E

13.   Answer: A B [C] D E

14.

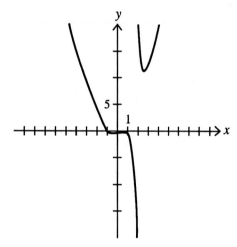

15.   Answer: [A] B C D E
16.   Answer: [A] B C D E

Chapter 5 Test–Form A

Directions:

Show all work where appropriate. Circle the **best** answer for each multiple-choice question. A graphing calculator may be necessary to answer some questions.

Each problem is worth 6 points. Scores can range from 4 through 100 points.

(5.4) 1.   Compute $\log_3 81$.

    A.   27

    B.   9

    C.   4

    D.   3

    E.   None of the above.

(5.4) 2.   Solve for x. $\log_x 4 = 1$

    A.   4

    B.   1

    C. $\dfrac{1}{4}$

    D.   0

    E.   None of the above.

(5.4) 3.   Solve for x. $\log_4 x = -3$

    A.   64

    B. -12

    C. -16

    D. -64

    E.   None of the above.

(5.2) 4.   What is the total value after 7 years of an initial investment of $2250 that earns interest at the rate of 6%, compounded monthly?

    A. $300,521.26

    B. $3420.83

    C. $3383.17

    D. $2388.78

    E. $2329.94

(5.5) 5.   The graph of $y = 3 + 2\log_a(x - 4)$ for $a > 1$ is best represented by which graph?

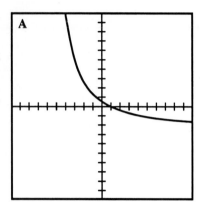

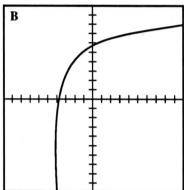

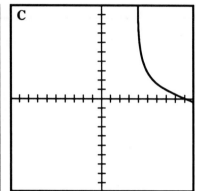

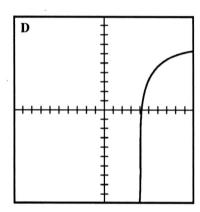

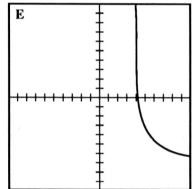

(5.1) 6.   A single cell amoeba doubles every 3 days. How long would it take one amoeba to produce a population of about 10,000 amoebae?

   A.   1667 days

   B.   333 days

   C.   126 days

   D.   40 days

   E.   13 days

(5.1) 7.   Solve for x: $3^{2x-1} = 27$.

(5.5) 8.   The graph of $y = 2 - a^{3-x}$ for $a > 1$ is best represented by which graph?

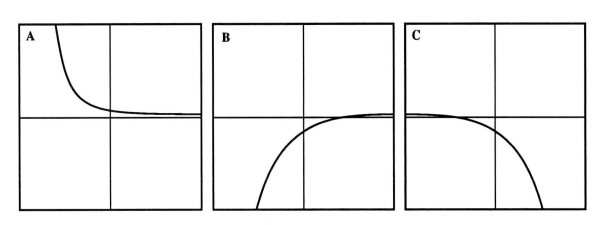

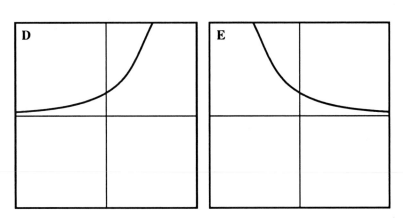

(5.6) 9.   Let $S = a(1.08)^t$. Solve for t.

A. $\dfrac{\ln a - \ln S}{\ln 1.08}$

B. $\dfrac{\ln(1.08)}{\ln a + \ln S}$

C. $\ln a + \ln 1.08$

D. $\dfrac{\ln\left(\dfrac{S}{a}\right)}{\ln 1.08}$

E.   None of the above.

(5.5) 10. Which of the following is the best graph of $f(x) = \begin{cases} x^2 & \text{for } x \leq -1 \\ \log|x| & \text{for } x > -1 \end{cases}$?

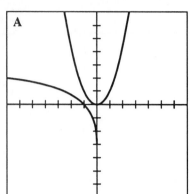

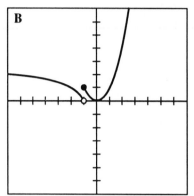

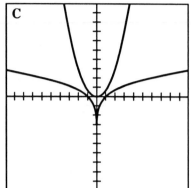

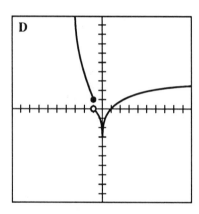

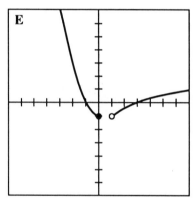

(5.3) 11. The effective annual rate of an account paying 6% compounded monthly is

A.   5.00%

B.   6.00%

C.   6.07%

D.   6.17%

E.   6.37%

(5.3) 12. Juana deposits $200 each month into a retirement account that pays 9.00% APR (0.75% per month). What is the value of this annuity after 30 years?

A. $366,148.70

B. $78,754.10

C. $78,480.00

D. $72,000.00

E. $24,856.37

(5.3) 13.   To finance their new home, the Tiballis have agrees to a $80,000 mortgage loan at 8.75% APR. What will their monthly payments be if the loan has a term of 20 years?

A. $746.97

B. $736.97

C. $726.97

D. $716.97

E. $706.97

In Problems 14–16, let $f(x) = 6xe^{-0.4x}$.

(5.6) 14.   Draw a complete graph of f .

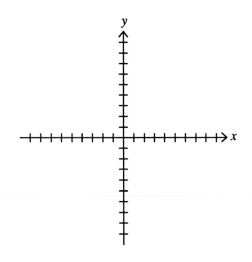

(5.6) 15.   Determine the x-coordinates where all maximum and minimum values occur.

A.   4.5

B.   2.5

C.   1.5

D.   0 and 5.5

E.   0 and 2

(5.6) 16.   Find the *sum* of the solutions to $f(x) = 3$. That is, find the solution(s); then *add* them.

A.   9

B.   7

C.   5

D.   3

E.   1

Chapter 5 Test–Form A

Answer Sheet

1.   Answer: A B [C] D E
2.   Answer: [A] B C D E
3.   Answer: A B C D [E]
4.   Answer: A [B] C D E
5.   Answer: A B C [D] E
6.   Answer: A B C [D] E
7.   Answer: $x = 2$
8.   Answer: A [B] C D E
9.   Answer: A B C [D] E
10. Answer: A B C [D] E
11. Answer: A B C [D] E
12. Answer: [A] B C D E
13. Answer: A B C D [E]
14.

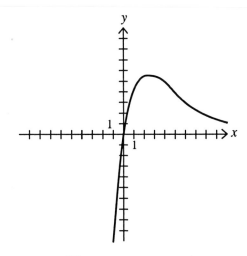

15. Answer: A [B] C D E
16. Answer: A [B] C D E

Chapter 5 Test–Form B

Directions:

Show all work where appropriate. Circle the **best** answer for each multiple-choice question. A graphing calculator may be necessary to answer some questions.

Each problem is worth 6 points. Scores can range from 4 through 100 points.

(5.4) 1. Compute $\log_4 64$.

    A. 60

    B. 16

    C. 3

    D. 1.204

    E. None of the above.

(5.4) 2. Solve for x. $\log_x 3 = 1$

    A. 0

    B. $\dfrac{1}{3}$

    C. 1

    D. 3

    E. None of the above.

(5.4) 3. Solve for x. $\log_5 x = -2$

    A. -10

    B. -25

    C. 10

    D. 25

    E. None of the above.

(5.2) 4. What is the total value after 6 years of an initial investment of $2250 that earns interest at the rate of 7%, compounded monthly?

    A. $3376.64

    B. $3420.24

    C. $3424.41

    D. $3472.16

    E. $3472.27

(5.5) 5.   The graph of $y = 3 + 2\log_a(x + 4)$ for $a > 1$ is best represented by which graph?

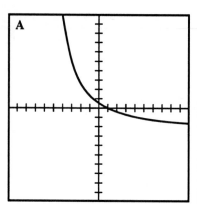 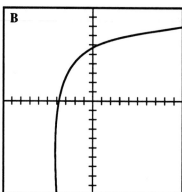 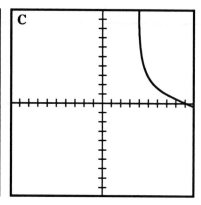

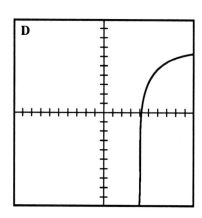 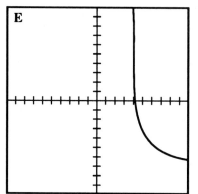

(5.1) 6.   A single cell amoeba doubles every 4 days. How long would it take one amoeba to produce a population of about 10,000 amoebae?

A.   1667 days

B.   333 days

C.   53 days

D.   40 days

E.   13 days

(5.1) 7.   Solve for x: $2^{3x-1} = 16$.

(5.5) 8.   The graph of $y = 2 - a^{x+3}$ for $a > 1$ is best represented by which graph?

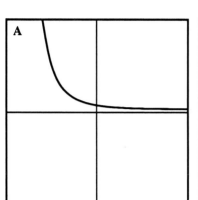
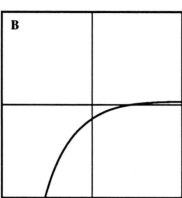
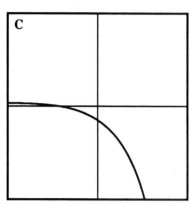

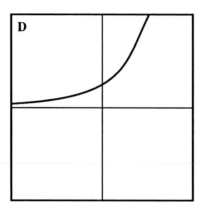
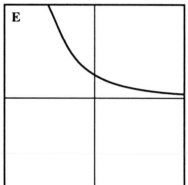

(5.6) 9.   Let $S = a(1.08)^t$. Solve for t.

A. $\dfrac{\ln S - \ln a}{\ln 1.08}$

B. $\dfrac{\ln(S - a)}{\ln 1.08}$

C. $\dfrac{\ln S}{\ln a} - \ln 1.08$

D. $\dfrac{\ln S}{\ln a \ln 1.08}$

E.   None of the above.

(5.5) 10.   Which of the following is the best graph of $f(x) = \begin{cases} x^2 & \text{for } x \geq -1 \\ \log|x| & \text{for } x < -1 \end{cases}$?

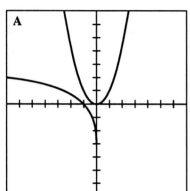

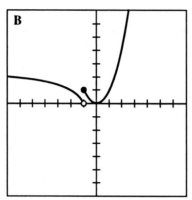

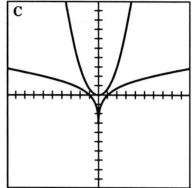

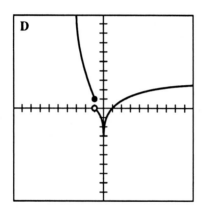

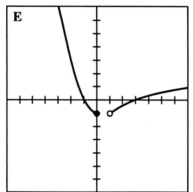

(5.3) 11.   The effective annual rate of an account paying 8% compounded quarterly is

    A.   7.00%

    B.   8.00%

    C.   8.12%

    D.   8.24%

    E.   8.36%

(5.3) 12.   Rosita deposits \$250 each month into a retirement account that pays 6.00% APR (0.50% per month). What is the value of this annuity after 20 years?

    A.   \$115,510.22

    B.   \$63,700.67

    C.   \$63,600.00

    D.   \$60,000.00

    E.   \$34,895.19

(5.3) 13.   To finance their new home, the Colemans have agreed to a $90,000 mortgage loan at 9.25% APR. What will their monthly payments be if the loan has a term of 15 years?

A. $966.27

B. $956.27

C. $946.27

D. $936.27

E. $926.27

In Problems 14–16, let $f(x) = 4xe^{-0.5x}$.

(5.6) 14.   Draw a complete graph of f.

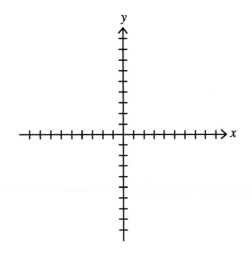

(5.6) 15.   Determine the x-coordinates where all maximum and minimum values occur.

A.   0 only

B.   2 only

C.   3 only

D.   0 and 2

E.   0 and 3

(5.6) 16.   Find the *sum* of the solutions to $f(x) = 2$. That is, find the solution(s); then *add* them.

A.   9

B.   7

C.   5

D.   3

E.   1

Chapter 5 Test–Form B

Answer Sheet

1.   Answer: A   B   C̲   D   E

2.   Answer: A   B   C   D̲   E

3.   Answer: A   B   C   D   E̲

4.   Answer: A   B̲   C   D   E

5.   Answer: A   B̲   C   D   E

6.   Answer: A   B   C̲   D   E

7.   Answer: $\dfrac{5}{3}$

8.   Answer: A   B   C̲   D   E

9.   Answer: A̲   B   C   D   E

10.   Answer: A   B̲   C   D   E

11.   Answer: A   B   C   D̲   E

12.   Answer: A̲   B   C   D   E

13.   Answer: A   B   C   D   E̲

14.

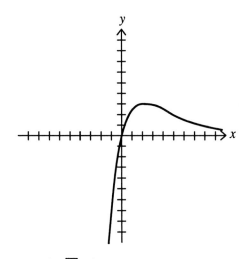

15.   Answer: A   B̲   C   D   E

16.   Answer: A   B   C̲   D   E

Chapter 6 Test–Form A

Directions:

Show all work where appropriate. Circle the **best** answer for each multiple-choice question. A graphing calculator may be necessary to answer some questions.

Each problem is worth 6 points. Scores can range from 4 through 100 points.

(6.2) 1. Let θ be an angle in standard position. Fnd the quadrant containing the terminal side of θ, if $\csc\theta < 0$ and $\sec\theta > 0$.

A. *I*

B. *II*

C. *III*

D. *IV*

E. None of the above.

(6.2) 2. Compute $\sin 128°$

A. 0.788

B. −0.613

C. 0.721

D. −0.692

E. −1.041

(6.2) 3. Compute $\sec 2$.

A. 0.909

B. 1.099

C. −2.402

D. −0.416

E. −2.185

(6.1) 4. Determine the length of an arc on the circumference of a circle of radius 5.5 subtended by a central angle of $25°$.

A. 137.50

B. 12.61

C. 4.98

D. 2.40

E. 2.32

In problems 5 and 6, let θ be an angle in standard position with $P = (-3, 4)$ on the terminal side of θ.

(6.2) 5. $\sin \theta =$

    A. $-\frac{3}{5}$

    B. $\frac{3}{5}$

    C. $-\frac{4}{5}$

    D. $\frac{4}{5}$

    E.   None of the above.

(6.2) 6. $\cot \theta =$

    A. $-\frac{3}{4}$

    B. $\frac{3}{4}$

    C. $-\frac{4}{3}$

    D. $\frac{4}{3}$

    E.   None of the above.

For problems 7 & 8, consider a right triangle ABC as shown in the figure.

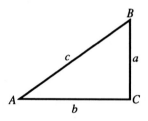

(6.5) 7.   Determine $\angle B$ if $c = 12.5$ and $b = 7$.

    A.   55.94°

    B.   34.06°

    C.   0.98°

    D.   52.85°

    E.   37.15°

(6.5) 8.   Determine a if $\angle B = 38°$ and $b = 4.5$.

    A.   27.24

    B.   3.52

    C.   2.77

    D.   3.55

    E.   5.76

(6.1) 9.   Determine the measure of an angle θ coterminal to an angle of $-40°$ if $360° \leq \theta \leq 720°$.

    A.   680°

    B.   400°

    C.   340°

    D.   500°

    E.   540°

(4.1) 10.   Determine θ if $\sin \theta = 0.375$ and $\frac{\pi}{2} \leq \theta \leq \pi$.

     A.   0.38

     B.   2.76

     C.   1.19

     D.   1.96

     E.   22.02

(6.3) 11.   A possible graph of $y = a - b\sin(x-1)$ for $a > b > 1$ is

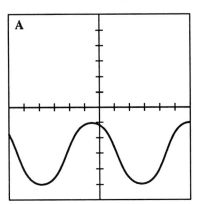 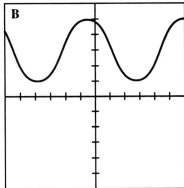 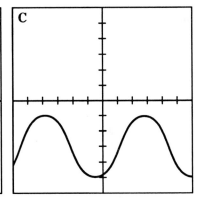

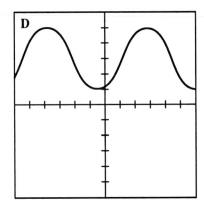 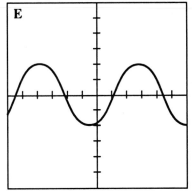

(6.3) 12.   The period of the function $f(x) = 3\sin \pi x$ is

     A.   3

     B.   2

     C.   1

     D. π

     E. $\frac{\pi}{2}$

(6.3) 13.   Solve graphically the inequality $\sin x > 0.3$ for $0 \le x \le 2\pi$.

Answer: _____

(6.4) 14.   The graph of $y = f(x)$ can be obtained from the graph of $y = \sec x$ by applying, in order, a horizontal stretch by a factor of 2, a vertical stretch by a factor of 3, and a vertical shift down 3 units. The equation of f is

A. $-3 + 3 \sec 2x$

B. $-3 + 3 \sec \frac{x}{2}$

C. $3 - 3 \sec 2x$

D. $3 - 3 \sec \frac{x}{2}$

E.   None of the above.

(6.2) 15.   A bicycle wheel of diameter 26 inches is rolled through an angle of $720°$. About how far has the wheel moved?

A.   52 inches

B.   82 inches

C.   41 inches

D.   163 inches

E.   327 inches

(6.6) 16.   The angle of elevation to the top of a building from a point 165 feet away from the building (on level ground) is $26°$. Determine the height of the building.

Chapter 6 Test–Form A

Answer Sheet

1. Answer: A B C $\boxed{\text{D}}$ E

2. Answer: $\boxed{\text{A}}$ B C D E

3. Answer: A B $\boxed{\text{C}}$ D E

4. Answer: A B C $\boxed{\text{D}}$ E

5. Answer: A B C $\boxed{\text{D}}$ E

6. Answer: $\boxed{\text{A}}$ B C D E

7. Answer: A $\boxed{\text{B}}$ C D E

8. Answer: A B C D $\boxed{\text{E}}$

9. Answer: $\boxed{\text{A}}$ B C D E

10. Answer: A $\boxed{\text{B}}$ C D E

11. Answer: A $\boxed{\text{B}}$ C D E

12. Answer: A $\boxed{\text{B}}$ C D E

13. Answer: $0.30 < x < 2.84$ or $(0.30, 2.84)$

14. Answer: A $\boxed{\text{B}}$ C D E

15. Answer: A B C $\boxed{\text{D}}$ E

16. 80.48 feet

Chapter 6 Test–Form B

Directions:

Show all work where appropriate. Circle the **best** answer for each multiple-choice question. A graphing calculator may be necessary to answer some questions.

Each problem is worth 6 points. Scores can range from 4 through 100 points.

(6.2) 1.   Let θ be an angle in standard position. Find the quadrant containing the terminal side of θ, if $\csc\theta < 0$ and $\sec\theta < 0$.

     A.   *I*

     B.   *II*

     C.   *III*

     D.   *IV*

     E.   None of the above.

(6.2) 2.   Compute $\sin 256°$

     A. -0.999

     B. -0.970

     C. -0.788

     D. -0.692

     E. -0.573

(6.2) 3.   Compute $\sec 3$.

     A. -1.010

     B. -0.990

     C. 0.999

     D. 1.001

     E. 7.086

(6.1) 4.   Determine the length of an arc on the circumference of a circle of radius 4.5 subtended by a central angle of $35°$.

     A.   4.52

     B.   3.60

     C.   2.75

     D.   2.40

     E.   2.32

In problems 5 and 6, let θ be an angle in standard position with $P = (-4, 3)$ on the terminal side of θ.

(6.2) 5. $\sin \theta =$

A. $-\frac{3}{5}$

B. $\frac{3}{5}$

C. $-\frac{4}{5}$

D. $\frac{4}{5}$

E.   None of the above.

(6.2) 6. $\cot \theta =$

A. $-\frac{3}{4}$

B. $\frac{3}{4}$

C. $-\frac{4}{3}$

D. $\frac{4}{3}$

E.   None of the above.

For problems 7 and 8, consider a right triangle ABC as shown in the figure.

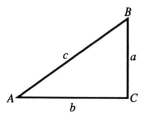

(6.5) 7.   Determine $\angle B$ if $c = 11.5$ and $b = 6.8$.

A.   32.96°

B.   34.06°

C.   35.37°

D.   36.25°

E.   37.15°

(6.5) 8.   Determine a if $\angle B = 43°$ and $b = 3.5$.

A.   1.76

B.   3.01

C.   3.26

D.   3.55

E.   3.75

(6.1) 9.   Determine the measure of an angle θ coterminal to an angle of $-80°$ if $360° \le \theta \le 720°$.

A.   680°

B.   640°

C.   540°

D.   500°

E.   340°

(6.3) 10.   Determine θ if $\sin\theta = 0.675$ and $\frac{\pi}{2} \le \theta \le \pi$.

     A.   2.40

     B.   2.23

     C.   1.89

     D.   1.38

     E.   0.74

(6.3) 11.   A possible graph of $y = a + b\sin(x-1)$ for $a < b < -1$ is

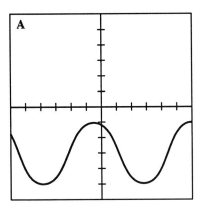
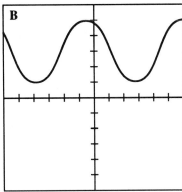
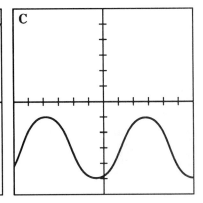

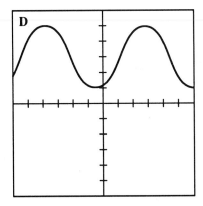
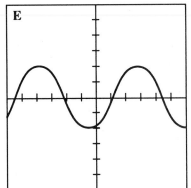

(6.3) 12.   The period of the function $f(x) = 3\sin(2\pi x)$ is

     A.   3

     B.   2

     C.   1

     D. π

     E. $\frac{\pi}{2}$

(6.3) 13.   Solve graphically the inequality $\sin x \leq 0.6$ for $0 \leq x \leq 2\pi$.

Answer: _____

(6.4) 14.   The graph of $y = f(x)$ can be obtained from the graph of $y = \tan x$ by applying, in order, a horizontal stretch by a factor of 2, a vertical stretch by a factor of 4, and a vertical shift down 3 units. The equation of f is

A. $3 - 4 \tan \frac{x}{2}$

B. $3 - 4 \tan 2x$

C. $-3 + 4 \tan \frac{x}{2}$

D. $-3 + 4 \tan 2x$

E.   None of the above.

(6.2) 15.   A bicycle wheel of diameter 66 cm is rolled through an angle of $720°$. About how far has the wheel moved?

A.   207 cm

B.   264 cm

C.   415 cm

D.   720 cm

E.   829 cm

(6.6) 16.   The angle of elevation to the top of a building from a point 55 meters away from the building (on level ground) is $39°$. Determine the height of the building.

Chapter 6 Test–Form B

Answer Sheet

1.   Answer: A B ☐C D E

2.   Answer: A ☐B C D E

3.   Answer: ☐A B C D E

4.   Answer: A B ☐C D E

5.   Answer: A ☐B C D E

6.   Answer: A B ☐C D E

7.   Answer: A B C ☐D E

8.   Answer: A B C D ☐E

9.   Answer: A ☐B C D E

10. Answer: ☐A B C D E

11. Answer: ☐A B C D E

12. Answer: A B ☐C D E

13. Answer: $[0, 0.64] \cup [2.50, 2\pi]$ or $[0.00, 0.64] \cup [2.50, 6.28]$

14. Answer: A B ☐C D E

15. Answer: A B ☐C D E

16. 44.54 feet

Mid-Year Test–Form A

Directions:

Show all work where appropriate. Circle the **best** answer for each multiple-choice question. A graphing calculator may be necessary to answer some questions.

Each problem is worth 4 points. Scores can range from 0 through 100 points.

(1.1) 1.   Show that the points $A(4,2)$, $B(-1,0)$, $C(-3,5)$, and $D(2,7)$ are the vertices of a rhombus.

(1.2) 2.   Which ONE of the following viewing rectangles gives the best *complete* graph of $y = 25x^3 - |2x|$?

    A. $[-10, 10]$ by $[-10, 10]$

    B. $[-1, 1]$ by $[-1, 1]$

    C. $[-1, 1]$ by $[-10, 10]$

    D. $[-10, 10]$ by $[-1, 1]$

    E. $[-5, 5]$ by $[-15, 15]$

(1.3) 3.   Determine the domain of the function $g(x) = |x^2 - 3x + 2|$.

    A. $[0, \infty)$

    B. $(-\infty, 0]$

    C. $(0, \infty)$

    D. $[2, \infty)$

    E. $(-\infty, \infty)$

(1.6) 4.   Let $f(x) = \sqrt{x-3}$ and $g(x) = x^2 + 1$. Compute $f \circ g$.

    A. $\sqrt{x^2 - 2}$

    B. $\sqrt{x^2 + 1}$

    C. $x - 2$

    D. $x^2 - 2$

    E. $x + 10$

(1.5) 5.   The following three transformations are applied (in the given order) to the graph of $y = x^2$:

    I.   A vertical stretch by a factor of 3.

    II. A horizontal shift right 5 units.

    III. A vertical shift down 6 units.

Which of the following is an equation for the graph produced as a result of applying these transformations?

    A. $y = 5x^2 - 1$

    B. $y = 3(x - 5)^2 - 6$

    C. $y = 3(x + 5)^2 - 6$

    D. $y = 3x^2 - 1$

    E. $y = 3(x - 6)^2 + 5$

(3.5) 6.   The complex number $2 + 3i$ is a zero of $f(x) = x^4 - 5x^3 + 15x^2 - 5x - 26$. Find all the other zeros of f.

    A. $x = 2 - 3i$

    B. $x = 1$ and $x = 2$

    C. $x = 2 - 3i$, $x = -2$, and $x = 1$

    D. $x = 2 - 3i$, $x = -1$, and $x = 2$

    E. $x = 2 - 3i$, $x = -3$, $x = -1$, and $x = 3$

(2.7) 7.   Let $f(x) = \dfrac{3x + 7}{x - 2}$. Find a rule for f^{-1}.

    A. $y = \dfrac{x - 2}{3x + 7}$

    B. $y = \dfrac{2x + 7}{x}$

    C. $y = \dfrac{2x + 7}{x - 3}$

    D. $y = \dfrac{x - 3}{2x + 7}$

    E. $y = \dfrac{2x + 7}{3 - x}$

(3.1) 8.   Find the interval(s) on which $f(x) = 0.5x^5 - 3x^3 + 7x^2 + 10$ is increasing.

    A. $(-\infty, -2.43) \cup (0, \infty)$

    B. $(-2.43, 0)$

    C. $(0, \infty)$

    D. $(-\infty, -2.43)$

    E. $(-\infty, \infty)$

(2.5) 9.   Solve $(x^2 + 3x - 2)(x + 5) \geq 0$.

    A. $[-5, -3.56]$

    B. $[0.56, \infty)$

    C. $[-3.56, 0.56]$

    D. $[-5, -3.56] \cup [0.56, \infty)$

    E.   None of the above.

(3.3) 10. Find a polynomial of degree 3 that has $3 + i$ and -7 as zeros.

    A. $x^3 - 6x^2 + 8x$

    B. $x^3 + x^2 - 34x + 56$

    C. $x^3 + x^2 - 32x + 70$

    D. $x^3 + x^2 - 52x - 70$

    E. $x^3 + 13x^2 - 32x + 70$

(3.2) 11. Identify the function(s) that are continuous:

    I. $f(x) = 3x^3 - 5x^2 + 10x - 3$

    II. $f(x) = \dfrac{2x^3 - 7x^2 - 4x}{x - 4}$

    III. $f(x) = \begin{cases} x, & x < 0 \\ x^2, & 0 \le x \le 1 \\ 2 - x, & x > 1 \end{cases}$

    A.   I only

    B.   II only

    C.   III only

    D.   I and III only

    E.   All the functions are continuous.

(4.1) 12. Find the *domain* of $g(x) = \dfrac{x^3 + 3}{x^2 - 3}$.

    A. $(-\infty, \infty)$

    B. $(-\infty, -\sqrt{3})$

    C. $(\sqrt{3}, \infty)$

    D. $(-\infty, -\sqrt{3}) \cup (\sqrt{3}, \infty)$

    E. $(-\infty, \sqrt{3}) \cup (\sqrt{3}, \infty)$

(4.1) 13. Find the *range* of $f(x) = \dfrac{2x + 7}{x^2 - x - 12}$.

    A. $(-\infty, \infty)$

    B. $(-\infty, -3)$

    C. $(-3, 4)$

    D. $(4, \infty)$

    E. $(-\infty, -3) \cup (-3, 4) \cup (4, \infty)$

(4.1) 14. Find the *vertical* asymptotes of $f(x) = \dfrac{5}{x^2 - 7x + 10}$.

    A. $x = 0$

    B. $x = 5$

    C. $x = 2$

    D. $x = 2$ and $x = 5$

    E. $x = 0$, $x = 2$, and $x = 5$

(4.2) 15.   Determine all local extrema of the function $g(x) = \dfrac{x^3 + 5}{x^2 + 5}$.

A. $x = \sqrt{5}$

B. $x = 0$

C. $x = 0.65$

D. $x = 0$ and $x = \sqrt{5}$

E. $x = 0$ and $x = 0.65$

(5.5) 16.   Determine where the function $f(x) = x^2 \ln x$ is increasing.

A. $(0.61, \infty)$

B. $(0, \infty)$

C. $(1, \infty)$

D. $(0, 0.61]$

E. $(0, 1]$

(5.5) 17.   Let $g(x) = \dfrac{x^3}{\ln x}$. Determine what $g(x)$ approaches as $x \to \infty$.

A.   8.16

B. $-\infty$

C. ∞

D.   0

E.   1

(5.6) 18.   Find the simultaneous solution to the system

$$\begin{cases} y = x^3 \\ y = \ln x \end{cases};$$

that is, solve $x^3 = \ln x$.

A. $x = 0$

B. $x = 0.69$

C. $x = 1$

D. $x = 4$

E.   There is no solution.

(6.3) 19.   What is the period of $y = \sin 3x$?

A. 2π

B. 6π

C. $\dfrac{2\pi}{3}$

D. $\dfrac{\pi}{6}$

E. 3π

(6.5) 20. Let θ be an acute angle such that $\cos\theta = \dfrac{5}{13}$. Find the value of $\tan\theta$.

A. $\dfrac{13}{5}$

B. $\dfrac{12}{5}$

C. $\dfrac{5}{12}$

D. $\dfrac{13}{12}$

E. $\dfrac{5}{13}$

(6.5) 21. Determine the exact value of $\sin\dfrac{\pi}{3}$.

A. 2

B. $\dfrac{\sqrt{3}}{2}$

C. $\dfrac{1}{2}$

D. $\dfrac{2\sqrt{3}}{3}$

E. $\sqrt{3}$

(6.3) 22. Find the amplitude of $y = 2 + 6\cos 3x$.

A. 6

B. 3

C. 2

D. $\dfrac{2\pi}{3}$

E. -2

(5.4) 23. Find $\log_6 216$.

A. 0

B. 1

C. 2

D. 3

E. -3

(2.4) 24. Solve the double inequality $-12 < \dfrac{5x-6}{2} < -7$.

A. $(6, 3)$

B. $(6, -3]$

C. $\left(-\dfrac{2}{5}, \dfrac{11}{15}\right)$

D. $(-4, -2)$

E. $(-6, -3)$

(4.4) 25. Find all real numbers x that are solutions to $\sqrt[3]{x^2 - 2x + 6} - 5 = 0$.

    A. $x = -9.95$

    B. $x = 11.95$

    C. $x = 1.19$

    D. $x = -9.95$ and $x = 11.95$

    E. $x = -9.95$, $x = 1.19$, and $x = 11.95$

Mid-Year Test–Form A

Answer Sheet

1. Sample answer: $AB = \sqrt{[4-(-1)]^2 + (2-0)^2} = \sqrt{5^2 + 2^2} = \sqrt{25+4} + \sqrt{29}$;

   $BC = \sqrt{[-1-(-3)]^2 + (0-5)^2} = \sqrt{2^2 + (-5)^2} = \sqrt{4+25} = \sqrt{29}$;

   $CD = \sqrt{[2-(-3)]^2 + (7-5)^2} = \sqrt{5^2 + 2^2} = \sqrt{25+4} = \sqrt{29}$;

   $AD = \sqrt{(4-2)^2 + (2-7)^2} = \sqrt{2^2 + (-5)^2} = \sqrt{4+25} = \sqrt{29}$;

   Since all four sides have the same length, the points are the vertices of a rhombus. (Note: Other proofs are possible; check students' work.)

2. Answer: A [B] C D E
3. Answer: A B C D [E]
4. Answer: [A] B C D E
5. Answer: A [B] C D E
6. Answer: A B C [D] E
7. Answer: A B [C] D E
8. Answer: [A] B C D E
9. Answer: A B C [D] E
10. Answer: A B [C] D E
11. Answer: A B C [D] E
12. Answer: A B C [D] E
13. Answer: [A] B C D E
14. Answer: A B C [D] E
15. Answer: A B C D [E]
16. Answer: [A] B C D E
17. Answer: A B [C] D E
18. Answer: A B C D [E]
19. Answer: A B [C] D E
20. Answer: A [B] C D E
21. Answer: A [B] C D E
22. Answer: [A] B C D E
23. Answer: A B C [D] E
24. Answer: A B C D [E]
25. Answer: A B C [D] E

Mid-Year Test–Form B

Directions:

Show all work where appropriate. Circle the **best** answer for each multiple-choice question. A graphing calculator may be necessary to answer some questions.

Each problem is worth 4 points. Scores can range from 0 through 100 points.

(1.1) 1.   Show that the points $A(1, -3)$, $B(-8, 1)$, $C(-4, 10)$, and $D(5, 6)$ are the vertices of a square.

(1.2) 2.   Which ONE of the following viewing rectangles gives the best *complete* graph of $f(x) = 0.25x^3 - |2x|$?

      A. $[-10, 10]$ by $[-10, 10]$

      B. $[-1, 1]$ by $[-1, 1]$

      C. $[-1, 1]$ by $[-10, 10]$

      D. $[-10, 10]$ by $[-1, 1]$

      E. $[-2, 2]$ by $[-2, 2]$

(1.3) 3.   Determine the range of the function $g(x) = |x^2 - 3x + 2|$.

      A. $[0, \infty)$

      B. $(-\infty, 0]$

      C. $(0, \infty)$

      D. $[2, \infty)$

      E. $(-\infty, \infty)$

(1.6) 4.   Let $f(x) = \sqrt{x - 3}$ and $g(x) = x^2 + 1$. Compute $g \circ f$.

      A. $\sqrt{x^2 - 2}$

      B. $\sqrt{x^2 + 1}$

      C. $x - 2$

      D. $x^2 - 2$

      E. $x + 10$

(1.5) 5.   The following three transformations are applied (in the given order) to the graph of $y = x^2$:

   I.   A vertical stretch by a factor of 0.3.
   II. A horizontal shift left 5 units.
   III. A vertical shift up 6 units.

   Which of the following is an equation for the graph produced as a result of applying these transformations?

   A. $y = 5x^2 - 1$
   B. $y = 0.3(x - 5)^2 - 6$
   C. $y = 0.3(x + 5)^2 + 6$
   D. $y = 3x^2 - 1$
   E. $y = 0.3(x - 6)^2 + 5$

(3.5) 6.   The complex number $1 - 4i$ is a zero of $f(x) = x^4 - 4x^3 + 18x^2 - 28x - 51$. Find all the other zeros of f.

   A. $x = 1 + 4i$
   B. $x = 1$ and $x = 3$
   C. $x = 1 + 4i$, $x = -1$, and $x = 3$
   D. $x = 1 + 4i$, $x = -3$, and $x = 1$
   E. $x = 1 + 4i$, $x = -2$, $x = 1$, and $x = 3$

(2.7) 7.   Let $f(x) = \dfrac{5x - 10}{3x - 2}$. Find a rule for f^{-1}.

   A. $y = \dfrac{3x - 5}{2x - 10}$

   B. $y = \dfrac{2x - 10}{x}$

   C. $y = \dfrac{2x - 10}{3x + 5}$

   D. $y = \dfrac{3x - 2}{5x - 10}$

   E. $y = \dfrac{2x - 10}{3x - 5}$

(3.1) 8.   Find the interval(s) on which $f(x) = 0.5x^5 - 3x^3 + 7x^2 + 10$ is decreasing.
   A. $(-\infty, -2.43) \cup (0, \infty)$
   B. $(-2.43, 0)$
   C. $(0, \infty)$
   D. $(-\infty, -2.43)$
   E. $(-\infty, \infty)$

(2.5) 9.   Solve $(x^2 + 3x - 2)(x + 5) \le 0$.
   A. $[-5, -3.56]$
   B. $(-\infty, -5]$
   C. $[-3.56, 0.56]$
   D. $(-\infty, -5] \cup [-3.56, 0.56]$
   E. $(-\infty, -5] \cup [0.56, \infty)$

(3.3) 10. Find a polynomial of degree 3 that has $8 + 2i$ and 5 as zeros.

    A. $x^3 - 16x^2 + 68x$

    B. $x^3 + 21x^2 - 148x + 340$

    C. $x^3 - 11x^2 + 12x + 340$

    D. $x^3 - 21x^2 + 148x - 340$

    E. $x^3 - 16x^2 + 68x + 73$

(3.2) 11. Identify the function(s) that are continuous:

    I. $f(x) = \dfrac{2x^2 - 7x - 4}{2x + 1}$

    II. $f(x) = \dfrac{1}{3x^3} - 5x^2 + 10x - 3$

    III. $f(x) = \begin{cases} x, & x < 0 \\ x^2, & 0 \le x \le 1 \\ 2 - x, & x > 1 \end{cases}$

    A.   I only

    B.   II only

    C.   III only

    D.   I and III only

    E.   All the functions are continuous.

(4.1) 12. Find the *range* of $g(x) = \dfrac{x^3 + 3}{x^2 + 3}$.

    A. $(-\infty, \infty)$

    B. $(-\infty, -\sqrt{3})$

    C. $(\sqrt{3}, \infty)$

    D. $(-\infty, -\sqrt{3}) \cup (\sqrt{3}, \infty)$

    E. $(-\infty, \sqrt{3}) \cup (\sqrt{3}, \infty)$

(4.1) 13. Find the *domain* of $f(x) = \dfrac{2x + 7}{x^2 - x - 12}$.

    A. $(-\infty, \infty)$

    B. $(-\infty, -3)$

    C. $(-3, 4)$

    D. $(4, \infty)$

    E. $(-\infty, -3) \cup (-3, 4) \cup (4, \infty)$

(4.1) 14. Find the *horizontal* asymptotes of $f(x) = \dfrac{5}{x^2 - 7x + 10}$.

    A. $y = 0$

    B. $y = 5$

    C. $y = 2$

    D. $y = 2$ and $y = 5$

    E. $y = 0$, $y = 2$, and $y = 5$

(4.2) 15. Determine all local extrema of the function $g(x) = \dfrac{x^3 + 7}{x^2 + 7}$.

    A. $x = -\sqrt{7}$

    B. $x = 0$

    C. $x = 0.66$

    D. $x = 0$ and $x = 0.66$

    E. $x = -\sqrt{7}$, $x = 0$, and $x = 0.66$

(5.5) 16. Determine where the function $f(x) = x^3 \ln x$ is decreasing.

    A. $(-\infty, \infty)$

    B. $(0, 0.72)$

    C. $(0, \infty)$

    D. $(0.72, \infty)$

    E.   The function is always *increasing*.

(5.5) 17. Let $g(x) = \dfrac{x^2}{\ln x}$. Determine what $g(x)$ approaches as x approaches 1 *from the left*.

    A. $-\infty$

    B. ∞

    C. 0

    D. 1

    E. 1.67

(5.6) 18. Find the simultaneous solution to the system

$$\begin{cases} y = x^2 - 3x \\ y = \ln x \end{cases};$$

that is, solve $x^2 - 3x = \ln x$.

    A. $x = 3.36$

    B. $x = 0.37$

    C. $x = 0.37$ and $x = 3.36$

    D. $x = 1.75$

    E.   There is no solution.

(6.3) 19. What is the period of $y = 3 \cos 5x$?

    A. 2π

    B. $\dfrac{2\pi}{5}$

    C. 5π

    D. $\dfrac{5\pi}{2}$

    E. 3π

(6.5) 20. Let θ be an acute angle such that $\sin\theta = \dfrac{24}{25}$. Find the value of $\tan\theta$.

  A. $\dfrac{24}{7}$

  B. $\dfrac{7}{24}$

  C. $\dfrac{7}{25}$

  D. $\dfrac{25}{7}$

  E. $\dfrac{25}{24}$

(6.5) 21. Determine the exact value of $\sin\dfrac{\pi}{4}$.

  A. $\dfrac{1}{2}$

  B. $\sqrt{2}$

  C. 1

  D. $\dfrac{\sqrt{3}}{2}$

  E. $\dfrac{\sqrt{2}}{2}$

(6.3) 22. Find the amplitude of $y = 3 + 5\cos 4x$.

  A. 3

  B. 4

  C. 5

  D. $\dfrac{\pi}{2}$

  E. -3

(5.4) 23. Find $\log_7 2401$.

  A. 1

  B. 2

  C. 3

  D. 4

  E. -3

(2.4) 24. Solve the double inequality $-8 < \dfrac{5x+4}{2} < 7$.

  A. $[-2, 4]$

  B. $(-4, 2)$

  C. $(2, 4)$

  D. $\left(-\dfrac{8}{5}, -\dfrac{1}{10}\right)$

  E. $(-4, -2)$

(4.4) 25.   Solve $\sqrt[3]{x^2 + 2x + 6} - 5 = 0$.

      A. $x = -9.95$

      B. $x = -11.95$

      C. $x = -9.95$

      D. $x = -11.95$ and $x = 9.95$

      E. $x = -11.95$, $x = -9.95$, and $x = 9.95$

Mid-Year Test–Form B

Answer Sheet

1.   Sample answer: $AB = \sqrt{[1 - (-8)]^2 + (-3 - 1)^2} = \sqrt{9^2 + (-4)^2} = \sqrt{81 + 16} + \sqrt{97};$
                       $BC = \sqrt{[-8 - (-4)]^2 + (1 - 10)^2} = \sqrt{(-4)^2 + (-9)^2} = \sqrt{16 + 81} = \sqrt{97};$
                       $CD = \sqrt{(-4 - 5)^2 + (10 - 6)^2} = \sqrt{(-9)^2 + 4^2} = \sqrt{81 + 16} = \sqrt{97};$
                       $AD = \sqrt{(1 - 5)^2 + (-3 - 6)^2} = \sqrt{(-4)^2 + (-9)^2} = \sqrt{16 + 81} = \sqrt{97};$
                       $m_{\overline{AB}} = \frac{1 - (-3)}{-8 - 1} = -\frac{4}{9}$ and $m_{\overline{BC}} = \frac{10 - 1}{-4 - (-8)} = \frac{9}{4}$, so $\overline{AB} \perp \overline{BC}$ since
                       $m_{\overline{AB}} \cdot m_{\overline{BC}} = -1.$ Since all four sides have the same length and since one pair of adjacent sides are perpendicular, the points are the vertices of a square. (Note: Other proofs are possible; check students' work.)

2.   Answer: [A]   B   C   D   E

3.   Answer: [A]   B   C   D   E

4.   Answer: A   B   [C]   D   E

5.   Answer: A   B   [C]   D   E

6.   Answer: A   B   [C]   D   E

7.   Answer: A   B   C   D   [E]

8.   Answer: A   [B]   C   D   E

9.   Answer: A   B   C   [D]   E

10.   Answer: A   B   C   [D]   E

11.   Answer: A   B   [C]   D   E

12.   Answer: [A]   B   C   D   E

13.   Answer: A   B   C   D   [E]

14.   Answer: [A]   B   C   D   E

15.   Answer: A   B   C   [D]   E

16.   Answer: A   [B]   C   D   E

17.   Answer: [A]   B   C   D   E

18.   Answer: A   B   [C]   D   E

19.   Answer: A   [B]   C   D   E

20.   Answer: [A]   B   C   D   E

21.   Answer: A   B   C   D   [E]

22.   Answer: A   B   [C]   D   E

23.   Answer: A   B   C   [D]   E

24.   Answer: A   [B]   C   D   E

25.   Answer: A   B   C   [D]   E

Chapter 7 Test–Form A

Directions:

Show all work where appropriate. Circle the **best** answer for each multiple-choice question. A graphing calculator may be necessary to answer some questions.

Each problem is worth 6 points. Scores can range from 4 through 100 points.

(7.4) 1. $(\csc \ x - \sec \ x)\sin x \cos x =$

      A. $\sin x - \cos x$

      B. $\cos x - \sin x$

      C. $\sin x + \cos x$

      D. $\cos x + \sin x$

      E.   None of the above.

(7.5) 2. $\cos(x - \pi) =$

      A. $\sin x \cos \pi + \cos x \sin \pi$

      B. $\sin x \cos \pi - \cos x \sin \pi$

      C. $\cos x \cos \pi + \sin x \sin \pi$

      D. $\cos x \cos \pi - \sin x \sin \pi$

      E.   None of the above.

(7.6) 3 – 4. Solve $\sin^2 x - \sin x = 0$ *algebraically*. Show all steps. Find *all* solutions in $[0, 2\pi]$. Give *exact* answers.

(7.1) 5.   Determine the <u>absolute</u> maximum *function value* of $f(x) = 7 \sin 2x \cos x$.

      A.   7

      B.   6.5

      C.   5.39

      D.   4.85

      E.   3.5

(7.1) 6.   Determine the intervals where $f(x) = 2\sin(0.5x)$ is decreasing in $(0, 4\pi)$.

    A. $(0, 4\pi)$

    B. $(0, 3\pi]$

    C. $(0, \pi] \cup [3\pi, 4\pi]$

    D. $(0, \pi] \cup [2\pi, 3\pi]$

    E. $[\pi, 2\pi]$

(7.4) 7.   Use algebraic means to verify the identity. $\cos x - \tan x = 2\cos 2x$.

(7.1) 8.   Determine all local minimum function values of $f(x) = 1 - 2\cos x$.

    A. 0

    B. -1

    C. -2

    D. -3

    E.   None of the above.

(7.3,7.6) 9.   Solve the inequality $\sin x \geq 1$.

    A. $(-1, 1)$

    B. $0, \frac{\pi}{2}, \frac{3\pi}{2}$

    C. $0, \pm\frac{\pi}{2}, \pm\pi, \pm\frac{3\pi}{2}, \pm 2\pi, \ldots$

    D. $x \geq \frac{\pi}{2}$, or $x \leq \frac{\pi}{2}$

    E.   None of the above.

(7.1) 10.   What is the range of $f(x) = 3\sin x + 2\cos x$?

    Range: _____

(7.2) 11.   Compute $\sin^{-1}(0.6)$.

    A. 0.56

    B. 0.64

    C. 1.78

    D. 1.56

    E. 0.54

(7.2) 12. Find an equivalent <u>algebraic</u> expression not involving trig functions for $\tan(\cos^{-1} u)$.

(7.1) 13. Determine the domain and range of $f(x) = 2 + 2\cos(x - \pi)$.

Domain: _____

Range: _____

(Review) 14. An end behavior model for $y = 3x \sin \dfrac{1}{x}$ is

A. $y = 0$

B. $y = 1$

C. $y = 3$

D. $y \to \infty$

E. $y \to -\infty$

(Review) 15. Determine what happens to the values of $f(x) = \dfrac{2\sin x}{x}$ as $x \to 0$.

A. $f(x) \to 0$

B. $f(x) \to 2$

C. $f(x) \to -2$

D. $f(x) \to \infty$

E. $f(x) \to -\infty$

(7.6) 16. Find *all* real solutions to the equation $2\sin x = x^3 - 4x$.

Solution:

Chapter 7 Test–Form A

Answer Sheet

1.   Answer: A [B] C D E

2.   Answer: A B [C] D E

3.   Answer:

$$\sin^2 x - \sin x = 0$$
$$\sin x(\sin x - 1) = 0$$
$$\sin x = 0 \ \text{ or } \ \sin x = 1$$

4.   Solutions: 0, $\frac{\pi}{2}$, π, 2π

5.   Answer: A B [C] D E

6.   Answer: A [B] C D E

7. $2\cot 2x = 2\left(\frac{\cos 2x}{\sin 2x}\right) = 2\left(\frac{\cos^2 x - \sin^2 x}{2\sin x \cos x}\right) = \frac{\cos x \cos x - \sin x \sin x}{\sin x \cos x} = \frac{\cos x \cos x}{\sin x \cos x} - \frac{\sin x \sin x}{\sin x \cos x} = \cot x - \tan x$

8.   Answer: A [B] C D E

9.   Answer: A B C D [E]

10. Range: $[-3.60, 3.60]$

11. Answer: A [B] C D E

12. Answer: $\frac{y}{x}$

13. Domain: all reals

     Range: $[0, 4]$

14. Answer: A B [C] D E

15. Answer: A [B] C D E

16. Answer: Solutions: 0, -2.18, 2.18

Chapter 7 Test–Form B

Directions:

Show all work where appropriate. Circle the **best** answer for each multiple-choice question. A graphing calculator may be necessary to answer some questions.

Each problem is worth 6 points. Scores can range from 4 through 100 points.

(7.4) 1. $(\sec x - \csc x)\sin x \cos x =$

    A. $\sin x - \cos x$

    B. $\cos x - \sin x$

    C. $\sin x + \cos x$

    D. $\cos x + \sin x$

    E.   None of the above.

(7.5) 2. $\sin(x - \pi) =$

    A. $\sin x \cos \pi + \cos x \sin \pi$

    B. $\sin x \cos \pi - \cos x \sin \pi$

    C. $\cos x \cos \pi + \sin x \sin \pi$

    D. $\cos x \cos \pi - \sin x \sin \pi$

    E.   None of the above.

(7.6) 3 – 4. Solve $2\cos^2 x - \cos x = 0$ *algebraically*. Show all steps. Find *all* solutions in $[0, 2\pi]$. Give *exact* answers.

(7.1) 5.   Determine the <u>absolute</u> maximum *function value* of $f(x) = 4\sin 2x \cos 3x$.

    A.   5.63

    B.   5.38

    C.   3.63

    D.   2.02

    E.   1.42

(7.1) 6.   Determine the intervals where $f(x) = \sin 2x$ is decreasing in $(0, \pi)$.

    A. $[0, \frac{\pi}{2}]$

    B. $[\frac{\pi}{2}, \pi]$

    C. $[0, \pi]$

    D. $[\frac{\pi}{4}, \frac{3\pi}{4}]$

    E. $[0, \frac{\pi}{4}] \cup [\frac{3\pi}{4}, \pi]$

(7.4) 7.   Use algebraic means to verify the identity: $\dfrac{\sin x}{1 + \cos x} = \dfrac{1 - \cos x}{\sin x}$.

(7.1) 8.   Determine all local minimum values of $f(x) = 3 - \sin x$.

    A.   0

    B.   1

    C.   2

    D.   3

    E.   None of the above.

(7.3,7.6) 9.   Solve the inequality $\cos 4x \geq 1$.

    A. $(-1, 1)$

    B. $0, \frac{\pi}{2}, \frac{3\pi}{2}$

    C. $0, \pm\frac{\pi}{2}, \pm\pi, \pm\frac{3\pi}{2}, \pm 2\pi, \ldots$

    D. $x \geq \frac{\pi}{2}$ or $x \leq \frac{\pi}{2}$

    E.   None of the above.

(7.1) 10.   What is the range of $f(x) = 3 \sin x + 4 \cos x$?

    Range: _____

(7.2) 11.   Compute $\cos^{-1}(0.4)$.

    A.   0.56

    B.   0.64

    C.   1.16

    D.   1.56

    E.   0.54

(7.2) 12.   Find an equivalent <u>algebraic</u> expression not involving trig functions for $\cos(\sin^{-1} u)$.

(7.1) 13.   Determine the domain and range of $f(x) = 3 + \sin(x + \pi)$.

Domain: _____

Range: _____

(Review) 14.   An end behavior model for $y = x \sin \dfrac{2}{x}$ is

    A. $y = 0$

    B. $y = 1$

    C. $y = 2$

    D. $y = x^2$

    E. $y = 2x^2$

(Review) 15.   What happens to the values of $f(x) = \dfrac{\sin x}{3x}$ as $x \to 0$.

    A. $f(x) \to 0$

    B. $f(x) \to \frac{1}{3}$

    C. $f(x) \to 3$

    D. $f(x) \to \infty$

    E. $f(x) \to -\infty$

(7.6) 16.   Find *all* real solutions to the equation $3 \sin x = x^3 - x$.

Solution:

Chapter 7 Test–Form B

Answer Sheet

1.   Answer: $\boxed{A}$ B C D E

2.   Answer: A $\boxed{B}$ C D E

3.   Answer: $2\cos^2 x - \cos x = 0$; $\cos x(2\cos x - 1) = 0$; $\cos x = 0$ or $2\cos x - 1 = 0$

4.   Solutions: $x = \frac{\pi}{2}, \frac{3\pi}{2}, \frac{\pi}{3}, \frac{5\pi}{3}$

5.   Answer: A B $\boxed{C}$ D E

6.   Answer: A B C $\boxed{D}$ E

7. $\frac{\sin x}{1+\cos x} \cdot \frac{1-\cos x}{1-\cos x} = \frac{\sin x(1-\cos x)}{1-\cos^2 x} = \frac{\sin x(1-\cos x)}{\sin^2 x} = \frac{1-\cos x}{\sin x}$

8.   Answer: A B $\boxed{C}$ D E

9.   Answer: A B $\boxed{C}$ D E

10.   Range: $[-5, 5]$

11.   Answer: A B $\boxed{C}$ D E

12.   Answer: $\sqrt{i - u^2}$

13.   Domain: all real numbers

      Range: $[2, 4]$

14.   Answer: A B $\boxed{C}$ D E

15.   Answer: A $\boxed{B}$ C D E

16.   Answer: $x = -1.67, 0, 1.67$

Chapter 8 Test–Form A

Directions:

Show all work where appropriate. Circle the **best** answer for each multiple-choice question. A graphing calculator may be necessary to answer some questions.

Each problem is worth 6 points. Scores can range from 4 through 100 points.

For Problems 1–5, consider the triangle ABC.

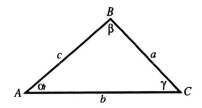

(8.1) 1. If $\alpha = 22°$, $\beta = 115°$, and $c = 12.75$, then $a =$

    A.   23.21

    B.   9.59

    C.   30.85

    D.   7.00

    E.   No such triangle exists.

(8.1) 2. If $a = 9$, $b = 8$, and $\alpha = 75°$, then $\beta =$

    A.   16.93°

    B.   120.84°

    C.   15.45°

    D.   164.55°

    E.   None of the above.

(8.2) 3. If $\alpha = 15.6°$, $b = 10.25$, and $c = 5.5$, then $a =$

    A.   124.45

    B.   26.72

    C.   5.17

    D.   11.16

    E.   No such triangle exists.

(8.2) 4. If $\alpha = 4$, $b = 5$, and $c = 6$, then $\gamma =$

    A.   82.82°

    B.   63.63°

    C.   55.77°

    D.   41.41°

    E.   38.38°

(8.2) 5. If $a = 8$, $b = 10$, and $\alpha = 67°$, then how many triangles are determined?

    A.   0

    B.   1

    C.   2

    D.   3

    E.   4

(8.3) 6. $(2 - 3i) + (-7 + 2i) =$

    A. $9 + 5i$

    B. $-5 + 5i$

    C. $-5 - i$

    D. $-14 + 6i$

    E. $-14 - 6i$

(8.3) 7. $3(\cos 30° + i \sin 30°) \cdot -4(\cos 20° + i \sin 20°) =$

    A. $-1(\cos 60° + i \sin 60°)$

    B. $-12(\cos 50° + i \sin 50°)$

    C. $-1(\cos 600° + i \sin 600°)$

    D. $-12(\cos 600° + i \sin 600°)$

    E. $-1(\cos 50° + i \sin 50°)$

(8.3) 8. A trigonometric representation of $-1 + \sqrt{3}i$ is

    A. $2(\cos 30° + i \sin 30°)$

    B. $2(\cos 60° + i \sin 60°)$

    C. $2(\cos 90° + i \sin 90°)$

    D. $2(\cos 120° + i \sin 120°)$

    E. $2(\cos 150° + i \sin 150°)$

(8.4) 9. $(-2 + 2i)^6$

    A. $6i$

    B. $8i$

    C. $12i$

    D. $-64i$

    E. $512i$

10. – 11. Let $\mathbf{u} = (3, 7)$ and $\mathbf{v} = (-2, 1)$ be vectors with initial point the origin.

(8.5) 10. $2\mathbf{u} + \mathbf{v} =$

    A. $(-4, 13)$

    B. $(4, 15)$

    C. $(-1, 9)$

    D. $(8, 15)$

    E. $(-12, 14)$

(8.5) 11. $|\mathbf{u} - \mathbf{v}| =$

    A. $\sqrt{89}$

    B. $\sqrt{65}$

    C. $\sqrt{37}$

    D. $\sqrt{61}$

    E.   None of the above.

(8.5) 12.   Let $A = (2, 5)$, $B = (-3, 6)$. Express the vector $\overrightarrow{AB}$ as a linear combination of $\mathbf{i} = (1, 0)$ and $\mathbf{j} = (0, 1)$.

13. – 14. Let $A = (-4, 3)$, $B = (1, 7)$, $C = (5, -2)$. **Express as a vector with initial point at the origin**

(8.5) 13. $2\overrightarrow{AB}$.

(8.5) 14. $\overrightarrow{AB} + \overrightarrow{AC} =$.

15. – 16. Given that $w = 5(\cos 20° + i \sin 20°)$ is one sixth root of a complex number z.

(8.4) 15.   List the other sixth roots of z.

(8.4) 16.   Determine z.

Chapter 8 Test–Form A

Answer Sheet

1. Answer: A B C $\boxed{\text{D}}$ E
2. Answer: A B C D $\boxed{\text{E}}$
3. Answer: A B $\boxed{\text{C}}$ D E
4. Answer: A B C $\boxed{\text{D}}$ E
5. Answer: $\boxed{\text{A}}$ B C D E
6. Answer: A B $\boxed{\text{C}}$ D E
7. Answer: A $\boxed{\text{B}}$ C D E
8. Answer: A B C $\boxed{\text{D}}$ E
9. Answer: A B C D $\boxed{\text{E}}$
10. Answer: A $\boxed{\text{B}}$ C D E
11. Answer: A B C $\boxed{\text{D}}$ E
12. Answer: $-5\mathbf{i} + \mathbf{j}$
13. Answer: $(10, 8)$
14. Answer: $(14, -1)$
15. Answer: $5 \operatorname{cis} \theta$ for $\theta = 80°$, $140°$, $200°$, $260°$, $320°$
16. $z = 15625 \operatorname{cis} 120°$

1

Chapter 8 Test–Form B

Directions:

Show all work where appropriate. Circle the **best** answer for each multiple-choice question. A graphing calculator may be necessary to answer some questions.

Each problem is worth 6 points. Scores can range from 4 through 100 points.

For Problems 1–5, consider the triangle ABC.

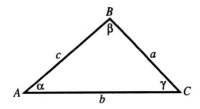

(8.1) 1.   If $\alpha = 25°$, $\beta = 112°$, and $c = 11.75$, then $a =$

     A.   23.21

     B.   9.59

     C.   30.85

     D.   7.28

     E.   No such triangle exists.

(8.1) 2.   If $a = 9$, $b = 8$, and $\alpha = 65°$, then $\beta =$

     A.   16.93°

     B.   53.67°

     C.   75.45°

     D.   164.55°

     E.   None of the above.

(8.2) 3.   If $\alpha = 15.6°$, $b = 11.25$, and $c = 5.5$, then $a =$

     A.   124.45

     B.   48.22

     C.   11.16

     D.   6.13

     E.   No such triangle exists.

(8.2) 4.   If $a = 4$, $b = 5$, and $c = 7$, then $\gamma =$

     A.   101.54°

     B.   78.46°

     C.   44.42°

     D.   34.05°

     E.   27.27°

(8.2) 5. If $a = 10$, $b = 8$, and $\alpha = 67°$, then how many triangles are determined?

    A.   0

    B.   1

    C.   2

    D.   3

    E.   4

(8.3) 6. $(2 - 3i) - (7 + 2i) =$

    A. $9 + 5i$

    B. $-5 - 5i$

    C. $9 - i$

    D. $-14 + 6i$

    E. $14 - 6i$

(8.3) 7. $2(\cos 40° + i\sin 40°) \cdot -3(\cos 20° + i\sin 20°) =$

    A. $-1(\cos 80° + i\sin 80°)$

    B. $-6(\cos 60° + i\sin 60°)$

    C. $-1(\cos 800° + i\sin 800°)$

    D. $-6(\cos 800° + i\sin 800°)$

    E. $-1(\cos 60° + i\sin 60°)$

(8.3) 8. A trigonometric representation of $-\sqrt{3} + i$ is

    A. $2(\cos 30° + i\sin 30°)$

    B. $2(\cos 60° + i\sin 60°)$

    C. $2(\cos 90° + i\sin 90°)$

    D. $2(\cos 120° + i\sin 120°)$

    E. $2(\cos 150° + i\sin 150°)$

(8.4) 9. $(1 + i)^{10} =$

    A. $32 + 32i$

    B. $10 + 10i$

    C. 10

    D. 32

    E. $32i$

10. – 11.   Let $u = (2, 5)$ and $v = (-2, 1)$ be vectors with initial point the origin.

(8.5) 10. $2u + v =$

    A. $(-4, 5)$

    B. $(4, 4)$

    C. $(0, 6)$

    D. $(-4, 4)$

    E. $(4, -4)$

(8.5) 11. $|u - v| =$

    A.   6

    B.   4

    C. $6\sqrt{2}$

    D. $4\sqrt{2}$

    E.   None of the above.

(8.5) 12.   Let $A = (5, 2)$, $B = (-2, 4)$. Express the vector $\overrightarrow{AB}$ as a linear combination of $i = (1, 0)$ and $j = (0, 1)$.

13. – 14.   Let $A = (-2, 1)$, $B = (3, 5)$, $C = (7, -1)$. Express as a vector with initial point at the origin

(8.5) 13. $2\overrightarrow{AB}$.

(8.5) 14. $\overrightarrow{AB} + \overrightarrow{AC} = .$

15. – 16.   Given that $w = 3(\cos 40^\circ + i \sin 40^\circ)$ is one sixth root of a complex number z.

(8.4) 15.   List the other sixth roots of z.

(8.4) 16.   Determine z.

Chapter 8 Test–Form B

Answer Sheet

1.   Answer: A B C $\boxed{\text{D}}$ E

2.   Answer: A $\boxed{\text{B}}$ C D E

3.   Answer: A B C $\boxed{\text{D}}$ E

4.   Answer: A B C $\boxed{\text{D}}$ E

5.   Answer: $\boxed{\text{A}}$ B C D E

6.   Answer: A $\boxed{\text{B}}$ C D E

7.   Answer: A $\boxed{\text{B}}$ C D E

8.   Answer: A B C D $\boxed{\text{E}}$

9.   Answer: A B C D $\boxed{\text{E}}$

10.   Answer: A B $\boxed{\text{C}}$ D E

11.   Answer: A B C $\boxed{\text{D}}$ E

12.   Answer: $-7\mathbf{i} + 2\mathbf{j}$

13.   Answer: $(10, 8)$

14.   Answer: $(14, 2)$

15.   Answer: $3(\cos\theta + i\sin\theta)$ for $\theta = 100^\circ, 160^\circ, 220^\circ, 280^\circ, 340^\circ$

16. $z = 3^6(\cos 240^\circ + i\sin 240^\circ)$

Chapter 9 Test–Form A

Directions:

Show all work where appropriate. Circle the **best** answer for each multiple-choice question. A graphing calculator may be necessary to answer some questions.

Each problem is worth 6 points. Scores can range from 4 through 100 points.

(9.2) 1. Determine polar coordinates of the point $(-2, 5)$.

A. $(\sqrt{29}, 1.19)$

B. $(\sqrt{21}, 1.19)$

C. $(\sqrt{29}, 1.95)$

D. $(\sqrt{29}, -1.19)$

E. $(\sqrt{29}, -1.95)$

(9.2) 2. Determine the rectangular coordinates of the point with polar coordinates $(8, 325°)$.

A. $(6.55, -4.59)$

B. $(-6.55, 4.59)$

C. $(4.59, -6.55)$

D. $(6.55, 4.59)$

E. $(4.59, 6.55)$

(9.2) 3. What is the minimum length of the interval that gives a complete graph of the polar equation $r = 2\sin 3t$?

A. π

B. 2π

C. 3π

D. 4π

E. None of the above.

(9.1) 4. What is the domain and range of the curve defined parametrically by $\begin{aligned} x(t) &= t\cos t \\ y(t) &= t\sin t \end{aligned}$ for $0 \le t \le 6.28$.

Domain: _____ Range: _____

(9.2) 5. If (x, y), a point in rectangular coordinates, is a solution to the polar system $\begin{cases} r &= 6\cos 3\theta \\ r &= 3\sin 3\theta \end{cases}$, where $0 \le \theta \le \frac{\pi}{4}$, then x could be

A. 2.1

B. 2.5

C. 2.7

D. 3.0

E. 3.3

6. – 8. An NFL punter at the 15 yard line kicks a football downfield with initial velocity 95 feet per second at an angle of elevation of 65°. Let t be the elapsed time since the football is kicked.

(9.3) 6.   a) Write a parametric equation representation of this problem situation.

   b) What values of t make sense in the problem situation?

(9.3) 7.   What is the distance the ball traveled in feet down field (to the nearest whole number)?

   A.   215
   B.   220
   C.   225
   D.   230
   E.   235

(9.3) 8.   What was the hang time in seconds?

   A.   5.1
   B.   5.2
   C.   5.3
   D.   5.4
   E.   5.5

(9.4) 9.   The focus of $x^2 = 16y$ is

   A. $(0, 2)$
   B. $(0, 4)$
   C. $(4, 0)$
   D. $(2, 0)$
   E.   None of the above.

(9.4) 10.   The equation of the directrix of $y^2 = 2x - 4$ is

   A. $x = \frac{3}{2}$
   B. $y = \frac{3}{2}$
   C. $x = -\frac{3}{2}$
   D. $y = -\frac{3}{2}$
   E.   None of the above.

(9.4) 11.   One of the foci of $2x^2 + y^2 = 4$ is

    A. $(0, \sqrt{2})$

    B. $(0, \sqrt{6})$

    C. $(\sqrt{2}, 0)$

    D. $(-\sqrt{6}, 0)$

    E.   None of the above.

(9.4) 12.   The center of $4x^2 + 9y^2 + 8x - 36y + 8 = 0$ is

    A. $(-1, 2)$

    B. $(1, -2)$

    C. $(-1, -2)$

    D. $(1, 2)$

    E.   None of the above.

(9.4) 13.   The center of $4x^2 + 4x - y^2 = 0$ is

    A. $(-1, 1)$

    B. $(-1, 0)$

    C. $(1, 1)$

    D. $(1, 0)$

    E.   None of the above.

(9.4) 14.   The asymptotes of $4x^2 - 9y^2 = 36$ are

    A. $y = \pm\frac{2}{3}x$

    B. $y = \pm\frac{3}{2}x$

    C. $y = \pm\frac{4}{9}x$

    D. $y = \pm\frac{9}{4}x$

    E.   None of the above.

(9.4) 15.   The graph of $y^2 + 2xy + 2x^2 - 4x = 0$ is

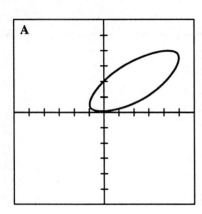

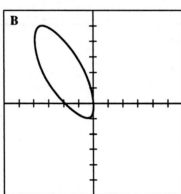

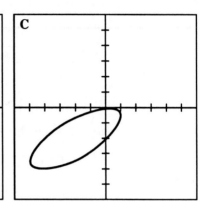

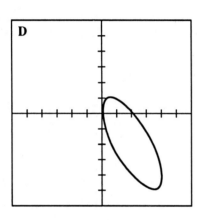

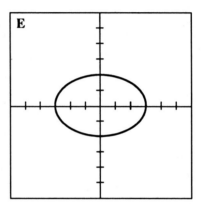

(9.5) 16.   The graph of the polar equation $r = \dfrac{4}{3 - 4\sin\theta}$ is a

A.   parabola opening up or down.

B.   parabola opening right or left.

C.   ellipse.

D.   hyperbola.

E.   None of the above.

Chapter 9 Test–Form A

Answer Sheet

1. Answer: A B $\boxed{C}$ D E
2. Answer: $\boxed{A}$ B C D E
3. Answer: A B C D $\boxed{E}$
4. Domain: $[-9.48, 9.48]$

   Range: $[-5.45, 7.91]$
5. Answer: A $\boxed{B}$ C D E
6. a) Answer: $x(t) = (95\cos 65°)t + 45$; $y(t) = (95\sin 65°)t - 16t^2$

   b) Answer: $0 \le t \le 5.42$
7. Answer: $\boxed{A}$ B C D E
8. Answer: A B C $\boxed{D}$ E
9. Answer: A $\boxed{B}$ C D E
10. Answer: $\boxed{A}$ B C D E
11. Answer: $\boxed{A}$ B C D E
12. Answer: $\boxed{A}$ B C D E
13. Answer: A B C D $\boxed{E}$
14. Answer: $\boxed{A}$ B C D E
15. Answer: A B C $\boxed{D}$ E
16. Answer: A B C $\boxed{D}$ E

Chapter 9 Test–Form B

Directions:

Show all work where appropriate. Circle the **best** answer for each multiple-choice question. A graphing calculator may be necessary to answer some questions.

Each problem is worth 6 points. Scores can range from 4 through 100 points.

(9.2) 1.　Determine polar coordinates of the point $(6, -3)$.

　　A.　$(6.71, -0.46)$

　　B.　$(-6.71, 0.46)$

　　C.　$(-0.46, 6.71)$

　　D.　$(-0.46, -6.71)$

　　E.　$(0.46, -6.71)$

(9.2) 2.　Determine the rectangular coordinates of the point with polar coordinates $(7, 162°)$.

　　A.　$(6.66, -2.16)$

　　B.　$(2.16, 6.66)$

　　C.　$(-6.66, 2.16)$

　　D.　$(-2.16, -6.66)$

　　E.　$(-2.16, 6.66)$

(9.2) 3.　What is the minimum length of the interval that gives a complete graph of the polar equation $r = 3 \sin 2\theta$?

　　A.　π

　　B.　2π

　　C.　3π

　　D.　4π

　　E.　None of the above.

(9.1) 4.　What is the domain and range of the curve defined parametrically by $\begin{aligned} x(t) &= \sin t \\ y(t) &= 2t \cos t \end{aligned}$ for $0 \le t \le 6.28$.

　　Domain: _____ Range: _____

(9.2) 5.　If (x, y), a point in rectangular coordinates, is a solution to the polar system $\begin{cases} r &= 3 \cos 3\theta \\ r &= 6 \sin 3\theta \end{cases}$, where $0 \le \theta \le \frac{\pi}{4}$, then x could be

　　A.　3.3

　　B.　3.0

　　C.　2.7

　　D.　2.4

　　E.　2.1

6. – 8.   An NFL punter at the 15 yard line kicks a football downfield with initial velocity 90 feet per second at an angle of elevation of $70°$. Let t be the elapsed time since the football is kicked.

(9.3) 6.   a) Write a parametric equation representation of this problem situation.

b) What values of t make sense in the problem situation?

(9.3) 7.   What is the distance the ball traveled in feet down field (to the nearest whole number)?

A.   163
B.   160
C.   157
D.   154
E.   151

(9.3) 8.   What was the hang time in seconds?

A.   5.1
B.   5.2
C.   5.3
D.   5.4
E.   5.5

(9.4) 9.   The focus of $y^2 = 16x$ is

A. $(0, 2)$
B. $(0, 4)$
C. $(4, 0)$
D. $(2, 0)$
E.   None of the above.

(9.4) 10.   The equation of the directrix of $x^2 = 2y - 4$ is

A. $x = \frac{3}{2}$
B. $y = \frac{3}{2}$
C. $x = -\frac{3}{2}$
D. $y = -\frac{3}{2}$
E.   None of the above.

(9.4) 11.   One of the foci of $x^2 + 2y^2 = 4$ is

    A. $(0, \sqrt{2})$

    B. $(0, \sqrt{6})$

    C. $(\sqrt{2}, 0)$

    D. $(-\sqrt{6}, 0)$

    E.   None of the above.

(9.4) 12.   The center of $4x^2 + 9y^2 + 8x + 36y + 8 = 0$ is

    A. $(-1, 2)$

    B. $(1, -2)$

    C. $(-1, -2)$

    D. $(1, 2)$

    E.   None of the above.

(9.4) 13.   The center of $4y^2 + 4y - x^2 = 0$ is

    A. $(1, -1)$

    B. $(0, -1)$

    C. $(1, 1)$

    D. $(0, 1)$

    E.   None of the above.

(9.4) 14.   The asymptotes of $9x^2 - 4y^2 = 36$ are

    A. $y = \pm\frac{2}{3}x$

    B. $y = \pm\frac{3}{2}x$

    C. $y = \pm\frac{4}{9}x$

    D. $y = \pm\frac{9}{4}x$

    E.   None of the above.

(9.4) 15.   The graph of $y^2 + 2xy + 2x^2 - 4x = 0$ is

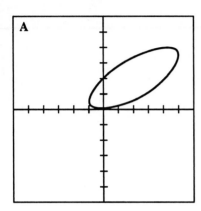

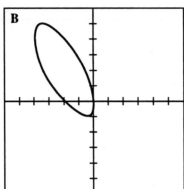

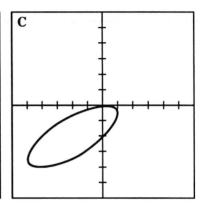

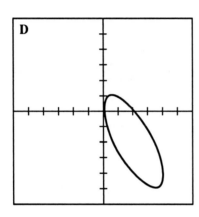

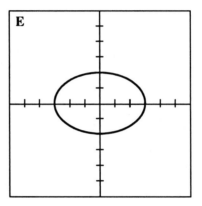

(9.5) 16.   The graph of the polar equation $r = \dfrac{3}{4 - 3\cos\theta}$ is a

A.   parabola opening up or down.

B.   parabola opening right or left.

C.   ellipse.

D.   hyperbola.

E.   None of the above.

Chapter 9 Test–Form B

Answer Sheet

1.   Answer: $\boxed{\text{A}}$ B   C   D   E

2.   Answer: A   B $\boxed{\text{C}}$ D   E

3   Answer: A   B   C   D $\boxed{\text{E}}$

4.   Domain: $[-1, 1]$

       Range: $[-6.58, 12.56]$

5.   Answer: A   B $\boxed{\text{C}}$ D   E

6.   a)   Answer: $x(t) = (90 \cos 70°)t$; $y(t) = -16t^2 + (90 \sin 70°)t$

       b)   Answer: $0 \le t \le 5.29$

7.   Answer: $\boxed{\text{A}}$ B   C   D   E

8.   Answer: A   B $\boxed{\text{C}}$ D   E

9.   Answer: A   B $\boxed{\text{C}}$ D   E

10.   Answer: A $\boxed{\text{B}}$ C   D   E

11.   Answer: A   B $\boxed{\text{C}}$ D   E

12.   Answer: A   B $\boxed{\text{C}}$ D   E

13.   Answer: A   B   C   D $\boxed{\text{E}}$

14.   Answer: A $\boxed{\text{B}}$ C   D   E

15.   Answer: A   B $\boxed{\text{C}}$ D   E

16.   Answer: A   B $\boxed{\text{C}}$ D   E

Chapter 10 Test–Form A

Directions:

Show all work where appropriate. Circle the **best** answer for each multiple-choice question. A graphing calculator may be necessary to answer some questions.

Each problem is worth 6 points. Scores can range from 4 through 100 points.

(10.1) 1.   Solve the following system of simultaneous equations for x :

$$2x - 5y = 6$$
$$4x - y = 3$$

   A. $x = -\dfrac{1}{2}$

   B. $x = -1$

   C. $x = \dfrac{1}{2}$

   D. $x = 1$

   E. None of the above.

(10.1) 2.   Use the substitution method to solve the system $\begin{array}{l} x - y = 4 \\ y = x^2 - 6 \end{array}$.

   A. $(1, -5)$, $(2, -2)$

   B. $(-1, -5)$, $(2, -2)$

   C. $(1, -5)$, $(2, 2)$

   D. $(-1, -5)$, $(2, 2)$

   E. $(1, 5)$, $(2, -2)$

(10.1) 3.   Use the elimination method to solve the system $\begin{array}{l} x^2 - 2y = -5 \\ x^2 + y = 4 \end{array}$.

   A. $(1, 3)$, $(1, -3)$

   B. $(-1, 3)$, $(-1, -3)$

   C. $(1, -3)$, $(-1, -3)$

   D. $(1, 3)$, $(-1, 3)$

   E. There are no simultaneous solutions.

(10.5) 4.   Find the number of simultaneous solutions to the system $\begin{array}{l} 2x - y^2 - 4 = 0 \\ y^2 - 4x^2 - 1 = 0 \end{array}$.

   A. 0

   B. 1

   C. 2

   D. 3

   E. 4

Problems 5, 6, and 7 refer to the system of equations

$$\begin{array}{rrrrl} 2x & - & 3y & + & z & = 7 \\ x & & & + & z & = 3 \\ 3x & - & y & - & z & = 2 \end{array}$$

(10.2) 5.   Write a matrix model of the system.

(10.2) 6.   Determine the *reduced row echelon* form of the matrix determined in Problem 6. List the
elementary row operations used in the proper order.

(10.2) 7.   Determine the solution $x = a$, $y = b$, and $z = c$ of the system. The *sum* $a + b + c$ is

A)   0

B)   1

C)   2

D)   3

E)   4

(10.2) 8. $\begin{pmatrix} 2 & 3 \\ 5 & 1 \end{pmatrix} \cdot \begin{pmatrix} 7 & 8 \\ 9 & 0 \end{pmatrix} =$

A. $\begin{pmatrix} 14 & 24 \\ 45 & 0 \end{pmatrix}$

B. $\begin{pmatrix} 14 & 45 \\ 24 & 0 \end{pmatrix}$

C. $\begin{pmatrix} 41 & 16 \\ 44 & 40 \end{pmatrix}$

D. $\begin{pmatrix} 41 & 44 \\ 16 & 40 \end{pmatrix}$

E.   None of the above.

(10.3) 9. The determinant of $\begin{pmatrix} 5 & -2 \\ 1 & 3 \end{pmatrix}$ is

    A.   17.

    B.   -17

    C.   7

    D.   -7

    E.   1

(10.3) 10. The inverse of $\begin{pmatrix} 2 & 3 \\ 6 & 4 \end{pmatrix}$ is

    A. $\begin{pmatrix} 0.4 & -0.3 \\ -0.6 & 0.2 \end{pmatrix}$

    B. $\begin{pmatrix} 0.2 & -0.6 \\ -0.3 & 0.4 \end{pmatrix}$

    C. $\begin{pmatrix} -0.4 & 0.3 \\ 0.6 & -0.2 \end{pmatrix}$

    D. $\begin{pmatrix} -0.2 & 0.6 \\ 0.3 & -0.4 \end{pmatrix}$

    E. $\begin{pmatrix} -0.2 & 0.3 \\ 0.6 & -0.4 \end{pmatrix}$

(10.5) 11. Find the simultaneous solution to the system $\begin{array}{l} x^2 - 4y^2 = 4 \\ y = 2x^2 - 3 \end{array}$.

    A.   (1.37, 0.73)

    B.   (-1.37, 0.73)

    C.   (1.04, -0.86)

    D.   (-1.04, -0.86)

    E.   There are no simultaneous solutions.

(10.5) 12. Sketch the graph of the inequality $4x^2 - 8x + 6y^2 + 24y + 4 < 0$.

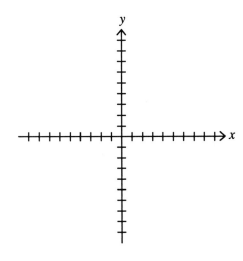

(10.2) 13.   Amy adds x cc of pure acid to 62 cc of a 42% acid solution. How much pure acid must be added so the mixture is 65% acid? Show your work.

(10.1) 14.   A school sold 2000 basketball tickets. There were two ticket prices: $3.50 for students and $5.00 for nonstudents. How many student tickets were sold if the total proceeds from the ticket sales were $8890?

    A.   600

    B.   640

    C.   680

    D.   720

    E.   None of the above.

(10.4) 15.   Suppose the graph of $y = x^2$ is rotated about the origin through an angle of $30°$. Which parametric equations would produce the rotated graph?

    A. $x' = \frac{\sqrt{3}}{2}t + \frac{1}{2}t^2,\ y' = \frac{1}{2}t + \frac{\sqrt{3}}{2}t^2$

    B. $x' = \frac{\sqrt{3}}{2}t + \frac{1}{2}t^2,\ y' = \frac{1}{2}t - \frac{\sqrt{3}}{2}t^2$

    C. $x' = \frac{\sqrt{3}}{2}t - \frac{1}{2}t^2,\ y' = \frac{1}{2}t - \frac{\sqrt{3}}{2}t^2$

    D. $x' = \frac{\sqrt{3}}{2}t - \frac{1}{2}t^2,\ y' = \frac{1}{2}t + \frac{\sqrt{3}}{2}t^2$

    E.   None of the above.

(10.4) 16.   Which matrix represents a rotation of $\dfrac{3\pi}{4}$ about the origin?

    A. $\begin{pmatrix} -0.7071 & -0.7071 \\ -0.7071 & -0.7071 \end{pmatrix}$

    B. $\begin{pmatrix} 0.7071 & -0.7071 \\ -0.7071 & -0.7071 \end{pmatrix}$

    C. $\begin{pmatrix} -0.7071 & 0.7071 \\ -0.7071 & -0.7071 \end{pmatrix}$

    D. $\begin{pmatrix} -0.7071 & -0.7071 \\ 0.7071 & -0.7071 \end{pmatrix}$

    E. $\begin{pmatrix} -0.7071 & -0.7071 \\ -0.7071 & 0.7071 \end{pmatrix}$

Chapter 10 Test–Form A

Answer Sheet

1.   Answer: A B $\boxed{C}$ D E

2.   Answer: A $\boxed{B}$ C D E

3.   Answer: A B C $\boxed{D}$ E

4.   Answer: $\boxed{A}$ B C D E

5.   Answer: $\begin{pmatrix} 2 & -3 & 1 & 7 \\ 1 & 0 & 1 & 3 \\ 3 & -1 & -1 & 2 \end{pmatrix}$

6.   Answer: Reduce to row echelon form:
$$\begin{pmatrix} 1 & 0 & 0 & 1 \\ 0 & 1 & 0 & -1 \\ 0 & 0 & 1 & 2 \end{pmatrix}$$
Elementary row operations (in order): $R_1 \leftrightarrow R_2$; $-R_1 + R_2$; $R_1 + R_3$; $-4R_2 + R_3$; $R_2 \leftrightarrow R_3$; $\frac{1}{11}R_2$; $R_1 \leftrightarrow R_3$; $3R_2 + R_1$; $-R_1 + R_3$

7.   Answer: A B $\boxed{C}$ D E

8.   Answer: A B $\boxed{C}$ D E

9.   Answer: $\boxed{A}$ B C D E

10.   Answer: A B $\boxed{C}$ D E

11.   Answer: A B C D $\boxed{E}$

12.

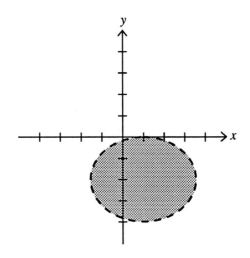

13.   Answer: $x = 40.74\,\text{cc}$

14.   Answer: A B C D $\boxed{\text{E}}$

15.   Answer: A B C $\boxed{\text{D}}$ E

16.   Answer: A B C $\boxed{\text{D}}$ E

Chapter 10 Test–Form B

Directions:

Show all work where appropriate. Circle the **best** answer for each multiple-choice question. A graphing calculator may be necessary to answer some questions.

Each problem is worth 6 points. Scores can range from 4 through 100 points.

(10.1) 1.   Solve the following system of simultaneous equations for y:

$$2x - 5y = 6$$
$$4x - y = 3$$

    A. $y = -\dfrac{1}{2}$

    B. $y = -1$

    C. $y = \dfrac{1}{2}$

    D. $y = 1$

    E.   None of the above.

(10.1) 2.   Use the substitution method to solve the system $\begin{array}{l} x - y = 3 \\ y = x^2 - 5 \end{array}$.

    A. $(1, -4)$, $(2, -1)$

    B. $(-1, -4)$, $(2, -1)$

    C. $(1, -4)$, $(2, 1)$

    D. $(-1, -4)$, $(2, 1)$

    E. $(1, 4)$, $(2, -1)$

(10.1) 3.   Use the elimination method to solve the system $\begin{array}{l} x^2 - y = -2 \\ x^2 + 2y = 7 \end{array}$.

    A. $(1, 3)$, $(1, -3)$

    B. $(-1, 3)$, $(-1, -3)$

    C. $(1, -3)$, $(-1, -3)$

    D. $(1, 3)$, $(-1, 3)$

    E.   There are no simultaneous solutions.

(10.5) 4.   Find the number of simultaneous solutions to the system $\begin{array}{l} 2x^2 - y - 2 = 0 \\ y^2 - 4x^2 - 1 = 0 \end{array}$.

    A.   0

    B.   1

    C.   2

    D.   3

    E.   4

Problems 5, 6, and 7 refer to the system of equations

$$\begin{array}{rcrcrcr} x & - & 2y & + & 2z & = & -1 \\ 2x & - & y & + & z & = & 2 \\ 3x & + & 2y & - & z & = & 9 \end{array}$$

(10.2) 5.   Write a matrix model of the system.

(10.2) 6.   Determine the *reduced row echelon* form of the matrix determined in Problem 6. List the
             elementary row operations used in the proper order.

(10.2) 7.   Determine the solution $x = a$, $y = b$, and $z = c$ of the system. The *sum* $a + b + c$ is

A)   0

B)   1

C)   2

D)   3

E)   4

(10.2) 8. $\begin{pmatrix} 2 & 5 \\ 3 & 1 \end{pmatrix} \cdot \begin{pmatrix} 7 & 9 \\ 8 & 0 \end{pmatrix} =$

A. $\begin{pmatrix} 54 & 29 \\ 18 & 27 \end{pmatrix}$

B. $\begin{pmatrix} 54 & 18 \\ 29 & 27 \end{pmatrix}$

C. $\begin{pmatrix} 41 & 16 \\ 44 & 40 \end{pmatrix}$

D. $\begin{pmatrix} 41 & 44 \\ 16 & 40 \end{pmatrix}$

E.   None of the above.

(10.3) 9.   The determinant of $\begin{pmatrix} 2 & 3 \\ 6 & 4 \end{pmatrix}$ is

    A.   10.

    B.   -10.

    C.   0.

    D.   18.

    E.   -18.

(10.3) 10.   The inverse of $\begin{pmatrix} 5 & -2 \\ 1 & 3 \end{pmatrix}$ is

    A. $\begin{pmatrix} 3 & 2 \\ -1 & 5 \end{pmatrix}$

    B. $\begin{pmatrix} 3 & -1 \\ 2 & 5 \end{pmatrix}$

    C. $\begin{pmatrix} 3 & 1 \\ 5 & 2 \end{pmatrix}$

    D. $\begin{pmatrix} 3 & 6 \\ -2 & 1 \end{pmatrix}$

    E.   None of the above.

(10.5) 11.   Find the simultaneous solution to the system $\begin{array}{c} x^2 - 4y^2 = 1 \\ y = 2x^2 - 2 \end{array}$.

    A.   (1.37, 0.73)

    B.   (-1.37, 0.73)

    C.   (1.04, -0.86)

    D.   (-1.04, -0.86)

    E.   None of the above.

(10.5) 12.   Sketch the graph of the inequality $4x^2 + 8x + 6y^2 - 24y + 4 < 0$.

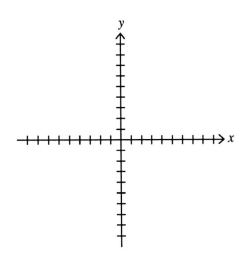

(10.2) 13.   Amy adds x cc of pure acid to 50 cc of a 12% acid solution. How much pure acid must be added so the mixture is 20% acid? Show your work.

(10.1) 14.   A school sold 2000 basketball tickets. There were two ticket prices: $3.50 for students and $5.00 for nonstudents. How many student tickets were sold if the total proceeds from the ticket sales were $8890?

    A.   620

    B.   660

    C.   700

    D.   740

    E.   None of the above.

(10.4) 15.   Suppose the graph of $y = x^2$ is rotated about the origin through an angle of $60^{\deg}$. Which parametric equations would produce the rotated graph?

    A. $x' = \frac{1}{2}t + \frac{\sqrt{3}}{2}t^2,\ y' = \frac{\sqrt{3}}{2}t + \frac{1}{2}t^2$

    B. $x' = \frac{1}{2}t + \frac{\sqrt{3}}{2}t^2,\ y' = \frac{\sqrt{3}}{2}t - \frac{1}{2}t^2$

    C. $x' = \frac{1}{2}t - \frac{\sqrt{3}}{2}t^2,\ y' = \frac{\sqrt{3}}{2}t - \frac{1}{2}t^2$

    D. $x' = \frac{1}{2}t - \frac{\sqrt{3}}{2}t^2,\ y' = \frac{\sqrt{3}}{2}t + \frac{1}{2}t^2$

    E.   None of the above.

(10.4) 16.   Which matrix represents a rotation of $\dfrac{5\pi}{4}$ about the origin?

    A. $\begin{pmatrix} -0.7071 & -0.7071 \\ -0.7071 & -0.7071 \end{pmatrix}$

    B. $\begin{pmatrix} 0.7071 & -0.7071 \\ -0.7071 & -0.7071 \end{pmatrix}$

    C. $\begin{pmatrix} -0.7071 & -0.7071 \\ 0.7071 & -0.7071 \end{pmatrix}$

    D. $\begin{pmatrix} -0.7071 & 0.7071 \\ -0.7071 & -0.7071 \end{pmatrix}$

    E. $\begin{pmatrix} -0.7071 & -0.7071 \\ -0.7071 & 0.7071 \end{pmatrix}$

Chapter 10 Test–Form B

Answer Sheet

1.   Answer: A B C   D   E

2.   Answer: A B C   D   E

3.   Answer: A   B   C D E

4.   Answer: A   B   C   D E

5.   Answer: $\begin{pmatrix} 1 & -2 & 2 & -1 \\ 2 & -1 & 1 & 2 \\ 3 & 2 & -1 & 9 \end{pmatrix}$

6.   Answer: $\begin{pmatrix} 1 & 0 & 0 & \frac{5}{3} \\ 0 & 1 & 0 & \frac{8}{3} \\ 0 & 0 & 1 & \frac{4}{3} \end{pmatrix}$

7.   Answer: A   B C D   E

8.   Answer: A B C   D   E

9.   Answer: A B C   D   E

10.   Answer: A   B   C   D E

11.   Answer: A   B   C   D E

12.

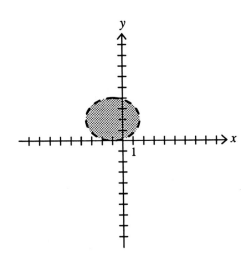

13.   Answer: 5 cc

14.   Answer: A B C $\boxed{\text{D}}$ E

15.   Answer: A B C $\boxed{\text{D}}$ E

16.   Answer: A B C $\boxed{\text{D}}$ E

Chapter 11 Test–Form A

Directions:

Show all work where appropriate. Circle the **best** answer for each multiple-choice question. A graphing calculator may be necessary to answer some questions.

Each problem is worth 6 points. Scores can range from 4 through 100 points.

(11.2) 1. Determine the *sum* of the first four terms of the sequence $\{a_n\}$ where $a_n = 3 - n^2$.

A) -11

B. -13

C. -15

D. -18

E. -20

(11.2) 2. Determine the sum, if it exists, of the infinite series

$$4 + \frac{4}{3} + \frac{4}{9} + \frac{4}{27} + \cdots$$

A. 6

B. 8

C. $\dfrac{16}{3}$

D. $\dfrac{22}{3}$

E. The sum does not exist.

(11.1) 3. The sequence $\{a_n\}$ is defined by $a_n = 2a_{n-1} + 3$ for $n \geq 2$ and $a_1 = -1$. Then the sixth term of the sequence $a_6 =$

A. -1

B. 0

C. 13

D. 29

E. 61

(11.1) 4. A sequence is defined by $a_n = 3a_{n-1} + 2$ for $n \geq 2$ and $a_1 = -1$. Then the sequence is

A. Arithmetic but not geometric.

B. Geometric but not arithmetic.

C. Both arithmetic and geometric.

D. Neither arithmetic nor geometric.

E. A Fibonacci sequence.

(11.2) 5.   The finite series $-1 + 2 + 7 + 14 + 23 + \cdots + 62 =$

A. $\displaystyle\sum_{k=1}^{8} (2k - 3)$

B. $\displaystyle\sum_{k=1}^{8} (k - 2)$

C. $\displaystyle\sum_{k=1}^{8} (2k^2 - 3)$

D. $\displaystyle\sum_{k=1}^{8} (k^2 - 2)$

E. $\displaystyle\sum_{k=1}^{8} (2k^2 + k - 4)$

(11.3) 6.   How many terms does $(a + b)^{100}$ have in expanded form?

A.   200
B.   101
C.   100
D.   99
E.   2

(11.3) 7.   The $x^3 y^2$ term of $(2x - 3y^2)^4$ has a coefficient of

A. -96
B. -216
C.   216
D.   96
E.   None of the above.

(11.6) 8.   The license plates in South Saskatoba consist of three letters followed by three digits with no repeated characters (letters or numbers) within each license plate. How many different license plates are possible?

A.   17,576,000

B.   15,600,000

C.   12,654,720

D.   11,232,000

E.   4,680,000

(11.6) 9.   A club with 14 members wishes to form a 3-member social committee. How many different committees are possible?

A.   2744

B.   2184

C.   728

D.   364

E.   27

(11.5) 10.   The principle of mathematical induction is used to show that a statement P_n holds true when n is any

   A.   real number

   B.   rational number

   C.   irrational number

   D.   integer

   E.   positive integer

(11.5) 11.   If the statement P_n is $1^2 + 2^2 + 3^2 + \cdots + n^2 = n(n+1)(n+2)/6$, then the statement P_{n+1} is

   A. $1^2 + 2^2 + 3^2 + \cdots + n^2 = n(n+1)(n+2)(n+3)/6$

   B. $2^2 + 3^2 + 4^2 + \cdots + (n+1)^2 = n(n+1)(n+2)(n+3)/6$

   C. $2^2 + 3^2 + 4^2 + \cdots + (n+1)^2 = (n+1)(n+2)(n+3)/6$

   D. $1^2 + 2^2 + 3^2 + \cdots + (n+1)^2 = (n+1)(n+2)(n+3)/6$

   E.   None of the above.

   In Problems 12 and 13 let $f_n(x) = 1 - \dfrac{x^2}{2!} + \dfrac{x^4}{4!} + \cdots + \dfrac{(-1)^n x^{2n}}{(2n)!}$.

(11.4) 12.   Compute $f_3(1)$.

   A.   0.54166...

   B.   0.50295...

   C.   0.50877...

   D.   0.54027...

   E.   0.54305...

(11.5) 13.   Based on a $[-10, 10]$ by $[-2, 2]$ viewing rectangle, the largest interval that $f_3(x)$ is a good approximation of $g(x) = \cos x$

   A. $[-1.5, 1.5]$

   B. $[-2.5, 2.5]$

   C. $[-3.5, 3.5]$

   D. $[-4.5, 4.5]$

   E. $[-5.5, 5.5]$

(11.7) 14.   The distance between $(-2, 3, 1)$ and $(0, 2, -5)$ with error less than 0.01 is

   A.   6.30

   B.   6.40

   C.   6.50

   D.   6.60

   E.   6.70

(11.7) 15.   An equation in parametric form for the line through $(-1, 2, 3)$ and $(2, 4, -2)$ is

    A. $x = 3t - 1, \ y = 2t + 2, \ z = -5t + 3$

    B. $\dfrac{x+1}{2} = \dfrac{y-2}{4} = \dfrac{x-3}{-2}$

    C. $x = -t + 2, \ y = 2t + 4, \ z = 3t - 2$

    D. $x = 2t + 1, \ y = 4t - 2, \ z = -2t - 3$

    E.   None of the above.

(11.8) 16.   The domain of $f(x, y) = \sqrt{4 - x^2 - y^2}$ is

    A.   All ordered pairs (x, y) such that $|x| \leq 2$ and $|y| \leq 2$.

    B.   All ordered pairs (x, y) such that $x^2 + y^2 \leq 4$.

    C.   All ordered pairs (x, y) such that $|x| \leq 4$ and $|y| \leq 4$.

    D.   All ordered pairs (x, y) such that both x and y are real.

    E.   None of the above.

Chapter 11 Test–Form A

Answer Sheet

1. Answer: A B C $\boxed{\text{D}}$ E
2. Answer: $\boxed{\text{A}}$ B C D E
3. Answer: A B C D $\boxed{\text{E}}$
4. Answer: A B $\boxed{\text{C}}$ D E
5. Answer: A B C $\boxed{\text{D}}$ E
6. Answer: A $\boxed{\text{B}}$ C D E
7. Answer: $\boxed{\text{A}}$ B C D E
8. Answer: A B C $\boxed{\text{D}}$ E
9. Answer: A B C $\boxed{\text{D}}$ E
10. Answer: A B C D $\boxed{\text{E}}$
11. Answer: A B C $\boxed{\text{D}}$ E
12. Answer: A B C $\boxed{\text{D}}$ E
13. Answer: A $\boxed{\text{B}}$ C D E
14. Answer: A $\boxed{\text{B}}$ C D E
15. Answer: $\boxed{\text{A}}$ B C D E
16. Answer: A $\boxed{\text{B}}$ C D E

Chapter 11 Test–Form B

Directions:

Show all work where appropriate. Circle the **best** answer for each multiple-choice question. A graphing calculator may be necessary to answer some questions.

Each problem is worth 6 points. Scores can range from 4 through 100 points.

(11.2) 1. Determine the *sum* of the first four terms of the sequence $\{a_n\}$ where $a_n = 1 + 2n^2$.

      A)   42

      B.   61

      C.   64

      D.   112

      E.   115

(11.2) 2. Determine the sum, if it exists, of the infinite series

$$\frac{1}{9} + \frac{4}{27} + \frac{16}{81} + \frac{64}{243} + \cdots$$

      A. $\dfrac{1}{21}$

      B. $\dfrac{1}{3}$

      C.   3

      D.   21

      E.   The sum does not exist.

(11.1) 3. The sequence $\{a_n\}$ is defined by $a_n = 3a_{n-1} + 2$ for $n \geq 2$ and $a_1 = -1$. Then the sixth term of the sequence $a_6 =$

      A. -1

      B.   0

      C.   13

      D.   29

      E.   61

(11.1) 4. A sequence is defined by $a_n = 2a_{n-1} + 3$ for $n \geq 2$ and $a_1 = -1$. Then the sequence is

      A.   Arithmetic but not geometric.

      B.   Geometric but not arithmetic.

      C.   Both arithmetic and geometric.

      D.   Neither arithmetic nor geometric.

      E.   A Fibonacci sequence.

(11.2) 5.   The finite series $-2 + 1 + 6 + 13 + 22 + \cdots + 61 =$

A. $\sum_{k=1}^{8} (2k - 4)$

B. $\sum_{k=1}^{8} (k - 3)$

C. $\sum_{k=1}^{8} (2k^2 - 4)$

D. $\sum_{k=1}^{8} (k^2 - 3)$

E. $\sum_{k=1}^{8} (2k^2 + k - 5)$

(11.3) 6.   How many terms does $(a + b)^{99}$ have in expanded form?

A.   198
B.   101
C.   100
D.   99
E.   2

(11.3) 7.   The $x^3 y^2$ term of $(3x - 2y^2)^4$ has a coefficient of

A. -96
B. -216
C.   216
D.   96
E.   None of the above.

(11.6) 8.   The license plates in South Saskatoba consist of three letters followed by three digits with repeated characters (letters or numbers) allowed. How many different license plates are possible?

A.   17,576,000

B.   15,600,000

C.   12,654,720

D.   11,232,000

E.   4,680,000

(11.6) 9.   A club with 13 members wishes to form a 4-member social committee. How many different committees are possible?

A.   28,561

B.   17,160

C.   4290

D.   715

E.   256

(11.5) 10.   The principle of mathematical induction is used to show that a statement P_n holds true when n is any

   A.   real number

   B.   rational number

   C.   irrational number

   D.   integer

   E.   positive integer

(11.5) 11.   If the statement P_n is $1^2 + 2^2 + 3^2 + \cdots + n^2 = n(n+1)(n+2)/6$, then the statement P_{n+1} is

   A. $1^2 + 2^2 + 3^2 + \cdots + n^2 = n(n+1)(n+2)(n+3)/6$

   B. $2^2 + 3^2 + 4^2 + \cdots + (n+1)^2 = n(n+1)(n+2)(n+3)/6$

   C. $2^2 + 3^2 + 4^2 + \cdots + (n+1)^2 = (n+1)(n+2)(n+3)/6$

   D. $1^2 + 2^2 + 3^2 + \cdots + (n+1)^2 = (n+1)(n+2)(n+3)/6$

   E.   None of the above.

In Problems 12 and 13 let $f_n(x) = x - \dfrac{x^3}{3!} + \dfrac{x^5}{5!} + \cdots + \dfrac{(-1)^n x^{2n+1}}{(2n+1)!}$.

(11.4) 12.   Compute $f_2(1)$.

   A. $0.80166\ldots$

   B. $0.84166\ldots$

   C. $0.85333\ldots$

   D. $0.88333\ldots$

   E. $0.89999\ldots$

(11.5) 13.   Based on a $[-10, 10]$ by $[-2, 2]$ viewing rectangle, the largest interval that $f_2(x)$ is a good approximation of $g(x) = \sin x$ is

   A. $[-1.5, 1.5]$

   B. $[-2.5, 2.5]$

   C. $[-3.5, 3.5]$

   D. $[-4.5, 4.5]$

   E. $[-5.5, 5.5]$

(11.7) 14.   The distance between $(-2, 4, 1)$ and $(0, 1, -7)$ with error less than 0.01 is

   A.   8.47

   B.   8.57

   C.   8.67

   D.   8.77

   E.   8.87

(11.7) 15.   An equation in parametric form for the line through $(2, 0, -3)$ and $(2, 3, 1)$ is

      A. $x = 2 + t,\ y = 3t,\ z = -3 + 4t$

      B. $x = 2 + t,\ y = 1 + 3t,\ z = 1 - 4t$

      C. $x = 2,\ y = 3t,\ z = -3 + 4t$

      D. $x = 2,\ y = 3t,\ z = 1 - 4t$

      E.   None of the above.

(11.8) 16.   The domain of $f(x, y) = \sqrt{9 - x^2 - y^2}$ is

      A.   All ordered pairs (x, y) such that $|x| \leq 3$ and $|y| \leq 3$.

      B.   All ordered pairs (x, y) such that $x^2 + y^2 \leq 9$.

      C.   All ordered pairs (x, y) such that $|x| \leq 9$ and $|y| \leq 9$.

      D.   All ordered pairs (x, y) such that both x and y are real.

      E.   None of the above.

Chapter 11 Test–Form B

Answer Sheet

1. Answer: A B $\boxed{\text{C}}$ D E
2. Answer: A B C D $\boxed{\text{E}}$
3. Answer: $\boxed{\text{A}}$ B C D E
4. Answer: A B C $\boxed{\text{D}}$ E
5. Answer: A B C $\boxed{\text{D}}$ E
6. Answer: A B $\boxed{\text{C}}$ D E
7. Answer: A $\boxed{\text{B}}$ C D E
8. Answer: $\boxed{\text{A}}$ B C D E
9. Answer: A B C $\boxed{\text{D}}$ E
10. Answer: A B C D $\boxed{\text{E}}$
11. Answer: A B C $\boxed{\text{D}}$ E
12. Answer: A $\boxed{\text{B}}$ C D E
13. Answer: $\boxed{\text{A}}$ B C D E
14. Answer: A B C $\boxed{\text{D}}$ E
15. Answer: A B $\boxed{\text{C}}$ D E
16. Answer: A $\boxed{\text{B}}$ C D E

Chapter 12 Test–Form A

Directions:

Show all work where appropriate. Circle the **best** answer for each multiple-choice question. A graphing calculator may be necessary to answer some questions.

Each problem is worth 6 points. Scores can range from 4 through 100 points.

(12.1) 1. A box contains three red marbles and three blue marbles. A marble is selected and, without replacing the first marble, a second marble is selected. What is the probability that both marbles are red?

   A. $\frac{1}{3}$

   B. $\frac{1}{4}$

   C. $\frac{1}{5}$

   D. $\frac{3}{4}$

   E. $\frac{2}{3}$

(12.1) 2. A spinner is divided evenly into four sections, numbered 1, 2, 3, and 4. Find the probability of spinning a 2 and then a 3 on two consecutive spins of the spinner.

   A. $\frac{1}{16}$

   B. $\frac{1}{4}$

   C. $\frac{1}{2}$

   D. $\frac{5}{16}$

   E. $\frac{5}{8}$

(12.2) 3. How many different hands of five cards can be dealt from a standard deck of 52 cards?

   A. $_{52}P_5$

   B. $_{52}C_5$

   C. $5!$

   D. $52!$

   E. $47!$

(12.2) 4. Find the probabilty of obtaining exactly three heads in nine tosses of a fair coin.

   A. 0.012

   B. 0.984

   C. 0.164

   D. 0.002

   E. 0.041

(12.3) 5. Find the mean of the data set {35.5, 38.3, 39.9, 42.5, 45.5, 47.5, 49.3, 51.5, 35.5, 38.5, 42.6, 45.5, 47.7, 49.3, 51.6, 35.6, 38.5, 45.8, 47.8, 49.4, 51.6, 45.8, 47.8, 51.7, 45.9}.

    A.   42.625

    B.   47.5

    C.   45.905

    D.   45.812

    E.   44.824

(12.4) 6. The stem-and-leaf table below shows the daily high temperature, in °F, for a city during three weeks last summer. (The entry with stem 7 and leaf 2 means 72°F.) Find the lower quartile, Q_L, and the upper quartile, Q_U, for these data.

Stem	Leaf
7	2
8	1 1 2 2 3 3 4 5 5 8 8 9 9
9	1 1 1 2 4 5
10	2

    A. $Q_L = 79.5$ and $Q_U = 94.5$

    B. $Q_L = 82.5$ and $Q_U = 91$

    C. $Q_L = 82$ and $Q_U = 91$

    D. $Q_L = 83$ and $Q_U = 91$

    E. $Q_L = 82.5$ and $Q_U = 92$

(12.4) 7. Find the standard deviation of the data set {52, 65, 65, 69, 70, 75, 77, 86, 95}.

    A.   43

    B.   72.67

    C.   12

    D.   9

    E.   11.86

(12.5) 8. Determine by visual inspection the type of linear correlation, if any, that exists between the x and y quantities in the following data:

x	5	10	12	13	15	20
y	16	33	40	39	40	59

    A.   strong positive correlation

    B.   weak positive correlation

    C.   little or no correlation

    D.   weak negative correlation

    E.   strong negative correlation

(12.5) 9. Find the equation of the curve of best fit for the data set {(1, 50), (2, 60), (3, 72), (4, 86.4), (5, 103.68), (6, 124.416)}.

    A. $y = 31.00 + 14.79x$

    B. $y = 39.88 + 39.09 \ln x$

    C. $y = 41.67(1.2)^x$

    D. $y = 45.68x^{0.50}$

    E. $y = 40.55(1.19)^x$

(12.5) 10. The logarithmic pair (x, y) corresponds to the linear pair

    A. $(\log y, y)$

    B. $(\log x, \log y)$

    C. $(x, \log y)$

    D. $(\log x, y)$

    E. $(x, \log x)$

(12.2) 11. A random check of one item on an assembly line is done every hour. If the probability of finding a defective item is 0.001, what is the probability of finding no defective items for ten consecutive checks?

    A. $(0.001)^{10}$

    B. $(0.999)^{10}$

    C. $\dfrac{1}{10}$

    D. $\dfrac{1}{10^{10}}$

    E. $10(0.999)^{10}$

Questions 12 through 14 refer to the following data:

Data:	52	57	60	62	66	68
Frequency:	3	2	4	5	7	2

(12.3) 12. Find the median of the data.

    A.   23

    B.   16

    C.   66

    D.   61.65

    E.   62

(12.3) 13. Find the mean of the data.

    A.   63.45

    B.   60.95

    C.   66

    D.   61.65

    E.   62

(12.4) 14. Find the variance of the data.

    A.   4.88

    B.   23

    C.   23.79

    D.   5.37

    E.   28.81

(12.2) 15. Find the probability of obtaining exactly four heads in ten tosses of a fair coin.

A. $210\left(\frac{1}{2}\right)^{10}$

B. $\left(\frac{1}{2}\right)^{4}$

C. $5040\left(\frac{1}{2}\right)^{10}$

D. $4!\left(\frac{1}{2}\right)^{4}$

E. $10!\left(\frac{1}{2}\right)^{10}$

(12.1) 16. A red die and a green die are tossed. Find the probability that the sum of the dice is 5.

A. $\dfrac{1}{11}$

B. $\dfrac{5}{36}$

C. $\dfrac{2}{11}$

D. $\dfrac{1}{9}$

E. $\dfrac{1}{18}$

Chapter 12 Test–Form A

Answer Sheet

1.   Answer: A   B $\boxed{\text{C}}$ D   E

2.   Answer: $\boxed{\text{A}}$ B   C   D   E

3.   Answer: A $\boxed{\text{B}}$ C   D   E

4.   Answer: A   B $\boxed{\text{C}}$ D   E

5.   Answer: A   B   C   D $\boxed{\text{E}}$

6.   Answer: A $\boxed{\text{B}}$ C   D   E

7.   Answer: A   B   C   D $\boxed{\text{E}}$

8.   Answer: $\boxed{\text{A}}$ B   C   D   E

9.   Answer: A   B $\boxed{\text{C}}$ D   E

10.   Answer: A   B   C $\boxed{\text{D}}$ E

11.   Answer: A $\boxed{\text{B}}$ C   D   E

12.   Answer: A   B   C   D $\boxed{\text{E}}$

13.   Answer: A   B   C $\boxed{\text{D}}$ E

14.   Answer: A   B $\boxed{\text{C}}$ D   E

15.   Answer: $\boxed{\text{A}}$ B   C   D   E

16.   Answer: A   B   C $\boxed{\text{D}}$ E

Chapter 12 Test–Form B

Directions:

Show all work where appropriate. Circle the **best** answer for each multiple-choice question. A graphing calculator may be necessary to answer some questions.

Each problem is worth 6 points. Scores can range from 4 through 100 points.

(12.1) 1. A dime, a nickel, and a quarter are tossed at the same time. What is the probability that exactly two of the three coins lands heads?

    A. $\dfrac{1}{4}$

    B. $\dfrac{2}{3}$

    C. $\dfrac{5}{8}$

    D. $\dfrac{3}{8}$

    E. $\dfrac{1}{2}$

(12.1) 2. A box contains eight balls numbered 1 to 8. A ball is selected and then replaced. A second ball is drawn. What is the probability of drawing the numbers 2 and 7?

    A. $\dfrac{1}{8}$

    B. $\dfrac{1}{64}$

    C. $\dfrac{1}{4}$

    D. $\dfrac{1}{2}$

    E. $\dfrac{9}{16}$

(12.2) 3. How many different 4-member committees can be formed from an organization containing 35 members?

    A. $_{35}C_4$

    B. $_{35}P_4$

    C. $4!$

    D. $35!$

    E. $31!$

(12.2) 4. Find the probability of obtaining exactly three tails in eleven tosses of a fair coin.

    A. 0.027

    B. 0.656

    C. 0.328

    D. 0.492

    E. 0.081

(12.3) 5. Find the mean of the data set {2.6, 2.7, 2.9, 3.1, 4.1, 4.2, 3.2, 3.3, 3.6, 3.7, 3.7, 2.9, 2.7, 3.1, 4.1, 3.2, 2.8, 3.3, 4.2, 4.1, 3.5, 3.4, 2.8, 3.4, 3.4, 3.7}.

    A.   3.35

    B.   3.3

    C.   3.37

    D.   3.45

    E.   3.5

(12.4) 6. The stem-and-leaf table below shows the daily high temperature, in °F, for a city during three weeks last winter. (The entry with stem 2 and leaf 2 means 22°F.) Find the lower quartile, Q_L, and the upper quartile, Q_U, for these data.

Stem	Leaf
2	2 9
3	1 1 2 5 7
4	1 1 2 3 3 5 7 9
5	1 1 2 2 2 6

    A. $Q_L = 33.5$ and $Q_U = 51$

    B. $Q_L = 35$ and $Q_U = 51$

    C. $Q_L = 33$ and $Q_U = 51$

    D. $Q_L = 33.5$ and $Q_U = 52$

    E. $Q_L = 32$ and $Q_U = 52.5$

(12.4) 7. Find the standard deviation of the data set {62, 66, 66, 67, 71, 73, 77, 77, 83}.

    A.   6.76

    B.   21

    C.   71.33

    D.   6.38

    E.   9

(12.5) 8. Determine by visual inspection the type of linear correlation, if any, that exists between the x and y quantities in the following data:

x	5	10	12	13	15	20
y	40	25	20	15	10	0

    A.   strong positive correlation

    B.   weak positive correlation

    C.   little or no correlation

    D.   weak negative correlation

    E.   strong negative correlation

(12.5) 9. Find the equation of the curve of best fit for the data set {(1, 50), (2, 81), (3, 99), (4, 112), (5, 122), (6, 130.6)}.

    A. $y = 45.2 + 15.4x$

    B. $y = 49.89 + 44.88 \ln x$

    C. $y = 51.12(1.19)^x$

    D. $y = 52.84x^{0.53}$

    E. $y = 49.82 + 45 \ln x$

(12.5) 10.   The exponential pair (x, y) corresponds to the linear pair

     A. $(\log y, y)$

     B. $(\log x, \log y)$

     C. $(x, \log y)$

     D. $(\log x, y)$

     E. $(x, \log x)$

(12.2) 11.   A random check of one item on an assembly line is done every hour. If the probability of finding a defective item is 0.005, what is the probability of finding no defective items for ten consecutive checks?

     A. $10(0.005)^{10}$

     B. $\dfrac{1}{10^{10}}$

     C. $\dfrac{1}{10}$

     D. $(0.005)^{10}$

     E. $(0.995)^{10}$

Questions 12 through 14 refer to the following data:

Data:	52	57	60	62	66	68
Frequency:	3	2	4	5	7	2

(12.3) 12.   Find the mean of the data.

     A.   63.45

     B.   60.95

     C.   66

     D.   61.65

     E.   62

(12.3) 13.   Find the mode of the data.

     A.   23

     B.   16

     C.   66

     D.   61.65

     E.   62

(12.4) 14.   Find the standard deviation of the data.

     A.   4.88

     B.   23

     C.   23.79

     D.   5.37

     E.   28.81

(12.2) 15.   Find the probability of obtaining exactly six heads in ten tosses of a fair coin.

      A. $10!\left(\dfrac{1}{2}\right)^{10}$

      B. $\left(\dfrac{1}{2}\right)^{6}$

      C. $151{,}200\left(\dfrac{1}{2}\right)^{10}$

      D. $6!\left(\dfrac{1}{2}\right)^{6}$

      E. $210\left(\dfrac{1}{2}\right)^{10}$

(12.1) 16.   A red die and a green die are tossed. Find the probability that the sum of the dice is less than 5.

      A. $\dfrac{1}{6}$

      B. $\dfrac{5}{36}$

      C. $\dfrac{4}{11}$

      D. $\dfrac{5}{18}$

      E. $\dfrac{1}{9}$

Chapter 12 Test–Form B

Answer Sheet

1. Answer: A B C [D] E

2. Answer: A [B] C D E

3. Answer: [A] B C D E

4. Answer: A B C D [E]

5. Answer: A B [C] D E

6. Answer: [A] B C D E

7. Answer: A B C [D] E

8. Answer: A B C D [E]

9. Answer: A [B] C D E

10. Answer: A B [C] D E

11. Answer: A B C D [E]

12. Answer: A B C [D] E

13. Answer: A B [C] D E

14. Answer: [A] B C D E

15. Answer: A B C D [E]

16. Answer: [A] B C D E

End-of-Year Test–Form A

Directions:

Show all work where appropriate. Circle the **best** answer for each multiple-choice question. A graphing calculator may be necessary to answer some questions.

Each problem is worth 4 points. Scores can range from 0 through 100 points.

(7.1) 1.   Which transformation was <u>not</u> performed on $y = \cos x$ to obtain $y = -4\cos\left(2x + \dfrac{\pi}{3}\right)$?

    A.   Vertical stretch by a factor of 4.

    B.   Reflection through the x-axis.

    C.   Horizontal stretch by a factor of 2.

    D.   Horizontal shrink by a factor of $\dfrac{1}{2}$.

    E.   Horizontal shift left $\dfrac{\pi}{6}$ units.

(7.3) 2.   Find all solutions to the equation $3\sin^2 x + 0.5\cos 3x + 0.5 = 0$.

    A. $x = \pi$

    B. $x = \pi + 2\pi$

    C. $x = \pi \pm 2\pi$

    D. $x = \pi \pm 2k\pi$, where k is any integer.

    E. $x = \pi \pm k\pi$, where k is any integer.

(7.5) 3.   Find the range of the function $f(x) = \csc x^2$.

    A. $\left(1, \dfrac{\pi}{2}\right]$

    B. $[1, \infty)$

    C. $(-\infty, \infty)$

    D. $(-\infty, -1] \cup [1, \infty)$

    E. $\left[\dfrac{\pi}{2}, \infty\right)$

(7.6) 4.   Solve the equation $\cos^2 x \sin x - \sin x - \cos^2 x + 1 = 0$ over the interval $(0, 2\pi)$.

    A. $x = \dfrac{\pi}{2}$

    B. $x = \pi$

    C. $x = \dfrac{\pi}{4}$

    D. $x = \dfrac{\pi}{2}$ and $x = \pi$

    E. $x = \dfrac{\pi}{4}$, $x = \dfrac{\pi}{2}$, and $x = \pi$

(8.1) 5.   On the playground, José is standing 16 feet from George and Carmen is standing 22 feet from George. The measure of the angle formed by the lines joining José and George and José and Carmen is 33°. How far is José standing from Carmen?

A.   12.23 feet

B.   35.42 feet

C.   27.20 feet

D.   15.10 feet

E.   33.61 feet

(8.2) 6.   The lengths of two sides of a triangle are 5 feet and 13 feet. The measure of the angle formed by these two sides is 100°. Find the length of the third side.

A.   14.72 feet

B.   205.29 feet

C.   216.57 feet

D.   14.55 feet

E.   11.40 feet

(8.2) 7.   Find the area of triangle ABC if $a = 6$, $b = 10$, and $\gamma = 140°$.

A.   84.02 square units

B.   30 square units

C.   39.57 square units

D.   22.98 square units

E.   19.28 square units

(8.5) 8.   A plane is flying on a bearing 75° east of north at 600 mph. Express the velocity of the plane as a vector.

A. $(155.29, 579.56)$

B. $(579.56, 155.29)$

C. $(-155.29, 579.56)$

D. $(579.56, -155.29)$

E. $(0.26, 0.97)$

(9.1) 9.   Find parametric equations for the circle with its center at the origin and a radius of 7.

A. $x = 7 \cos t$ and $y = 7 \sin t$

B. $x = 7 \sin t$ and $y = 7 \cos t$

C. $x = \cos 7t$ and $y = \sin 7t$

D. $x = \dfrac{1}{7} \cos t$ and $y = \dfrac{1}{7} \sin t$

E. $x = 49 \cos t$ and $y = 49 \sin t$

(9.3) 10. A ball is thrown upward with an initial velocity of 35 ft/sec at an angle of elevation of 75°. Consider the position of the ball at any time t, where $t = 0$ when the ball is thrown. Neglect air resistance. Find the maximum height of the ball.

A. 960 feet

B. 9.06 feet

C. 33.81 feet

D. 17.86 feet

E. 9.49 feet

(9.4) 11. Find the vertex of the parabola $4x^2 - y - 24x + 33 = 0$.

A. $(12, -3)$

B. $(-4, -3)$

C. $(-3, -4)$

D. $(3, -3)$

E. $(-3, 3)$

(9.4) 12. An ellipse has major axis of length 12 along the x-axis and minor axis of length 10 along the y-axis, with its center at the origin. Determine the standard form of the equation of the ellipse.

A. $x^2 + y^2 = 30$

B. $x^2 + y^2 = 120$

C. $\dfrac{x^2}{36} + \dfrac{y^2}{25} = 1$

D. $\dfrac{x^2}{12} + \dfrac{y^2}{10} = 1$

E. $\dfrac{x^2}{6} + \dfrac{y^2}{5} = 1$

(10.1) 13. Find the simultaneous solutions to the following system:

$$x - 3z = 0$$
$$x - y = 4$$
$$x + 2y - z = 0$$

A. $(3, -1, 9)$

B. $(24, 20, 8)$

C. $(-1, 1, 3)$

D. $(1, 3, -1)$

E. $(3, -1, 1)$

(10.3) 14.   Write the following matrix equation as a system of linear equations:

$$\begin{pmatrix} 4 & 7 \\ -6 & 2 \end{pmatrix} \begin{pmatrix} x \\ y \end{pmatrix} = \begin{pmatrix} 3 \\ -5 \end{pmatrix}$$

A. $4x + 7y = 3$
      $-6x + 2y = -5$

B. $4x - 6y = 3$
      $7x + 2y = -5$

C. $4x + 2y = -5$
      $-6x + 7y = 3$

D. $4x + 7y = -5$
      $-6x + 2y = 3$

E. $4x - 6y = -5$
      $7x + 2y = 3$

(10.4) 15.   Write a matrix that could be used to describe a rotation of $45°$ in the clockwise direction.

A. $\begin{pmatrix} \cos 45° & -\sin 45° \\ \sin 45° & \cos 45° \end{pmatrix}$

B. $\begin{pmatrix} \cos 45° & -\sin 45° \\ \cos 45° & \sin 45° \end{pmatrix}$

C. $\begin{pmatrix} \cos(-45°) & -\sin(-45°) \\ \sin(-45°) & \cos(-45°) \end{pmatrix}$

D. $\begin{pmatrix} \cos(-45°) & \sin(-45°) \\ -\sin(-45°) & \cos(-45°) \end{pmatrix}$

E. $\begin{pmatrix} \sin(-45°) & \cos(-45°) \\ \sin(-45°) & \cos(-45°) \end{pmatrix}$

(10.5) 16.   Find the simultaneous solutions to the system

$$\frac{x^2}{4} + \frac{y^2}{9} = 1$$
$$y = x^2.$$

A. $(-1.44, 2.08)$
B. $(1.44, 2.08)$
C. $(1.44, -2.08)$
D. $(-1.44, 2.08)$ and $(1.44, 2.08)$
E. $(1.44, 2.08)$ and $(1.44, -2.08)$

(11.1) 17.   Determine the 25th term of the arithmetic sequence $5, 2, -1, -4, \ldots$.

A. -3
B. 5
C. -72
D. -25
E. -67

(11.2) 18. Determine the sixth partial sum of the geometric sequence 2, 10, 50, 250, ...

    A.   15,624

    B.   3906

    C.   7812

    D.   15,625

    E.   312

(11.3) 19. Find the fifteenth term of $(4x - 3y)^{27}$, where the leading term is considered the zeroth term.

    A. $\binom{27}{15}(4x)^{15}(-3y)^{12}$

    B. $\binom{27}{15}(4x)^{12}(-3y)^{15}$

    C. $\binom{27}{15}(4x)^{13}(-3y)^{14}$

    D. $\binom{27}{15}(4x)^{14}(-3y)^{13}$

    E. $\binom{27}{15}(4x)^{15}(-3y)^{27}$

(11.6) 20. How many committees of 4 people can be formed in an organization with 57 members?

    A.   57!

    B.   4!

    C. $_{57}P_4$

    D. $_{57}C_4$

    E.   57!4!

(11.7) 21. Find the distance between the points $P(2, 3, 5)$ and $Q(-1, 6, 0)$.

    A.   6.56

    B.   3.74

    C.   6.16

    D.   6.08

    E.   2.24

(12.1) 22. A red die and a green die are rolled. Find the probability of rolling a sum greater than 8.

    A. $\dfrac{5}{12}$

    B. $\dfrac{5}{18}$

    C. $\dfrac{7}{12}$

    D. $\dfrac{5}{36}$

    E. $\dfrac{1}{4}$

(12.2) 23. A fair coin is tossed six times. Find the probability of two or three tails occurring.

   A. $\dfrac{15}{64}$

   B. $\dfrac{5}{64}$

   C. $\dfrac{5}{16}$

   D. $\dfrac{35}{64}$

   E. $\dfrac{1}{3}$

(12.3) 24. Find the mean of the data set $\{8.3, 7.7, 8.4, 9.6, 9.1, 9.0, 7.3, 7.2, 10.1, 7.9\}$.

   A. 9.05

   B. 8.35

   C. 7.69

   D. 9.40

   E. 8.46

(12.4) 25. Find the standard deviation of the data set $\{15, 23, 19, 32, 40, 25, 30, 31, 27, 22\}$.

   A. 6.84

   B. 2.62

   C. 46.84

   D. 7.14

   E. 5.60

End-of-Year Test–Form A

Answer Sheet

1. Answer: A B [C] D E
2. Answer: A B C [D] E
3. Answer: A [B] C D E
4. Answer: A B C [D] E
5. Answer: A B C D [E]
6. Answer: [A] B C D E
7. Answer: A B C D [E]
8. Answer: A [B] C D E
9. Answer: [A] B C D E
10. Answer: A B C [D] E
11. Answer: A B C [D] E
12. Answer: A B [C] D E
13. Answer: A B C D [E]
14. Answer: [A] B C D E
15. Answer: A B [C] D E
16. Answer: A B C [D] E
17. Answer: A B C D [E]
18. Answer: A B [C] D E
19. Answer: A [B] C D E
20. Answer: A B C [D] E
21. Answer: [A] B C D E
22. Answer: A [B] C D E
23. Answer: A B C [D] E
24. Answer: A B C D [E]
25. Answer: [A] B C D E

End-of-Year Test–Form B

Directions:

Show all work where appropriate. Circle the **best** answer for each multiple-choice question. A graphing calculator may be necessary to answer some questions.

Each problem is worth 4 points. Scores can range from 0 through 100 points.

(7.1) 1.   Which transformation was <u>not</u> performed on $y = \sin x$ to obtain $y = -3\sin\left(2x + \frac{\pi}{3}\right)$?

    A.   Horizontal shift left $\frac{\pi}{6}$ units.

    B.   Horizontal shift left $\frac{\pi}{3}$ units.

    C.   Vertical stretch by a factor of 3.

    D.   Reflection through the x-axis.

    E.   Horizontal shrink by a factor of $\frac{1}{2}$.

(7.3) 2.   Find all solutions to the equation $3\cos^2 x + 0.5\sin 3x + 0.5 = 0$.

    A. $x = \frac{\pi}{2}$

    B. $x = \frac{\pi}{2}$ and $x = \frac{3\pi}{2}$

    C. $x = \frac{\pi}{2} + k\frac{\pi}{2}$, where k is any integer.

    D. $x = \frac{\pi}{2} \pm k\pi$, where k is any integer.

    E. $x = \frac{\pi}{2} \pm 2k\pi$, where k is any integer.

(7.5) 3.   Find the domain of the function $f(x) = \cot x^2$.

    A. $(-\infty, \infty)$

    B. $[0, \infty)$

    C.   All x except $x = \frac{\pi}{2} + k\pi$, where k is any integer.

    D.   All x except $x = \frac{\pi}{2} + 2k\pi$, where k is any integer.

    E.   All x except $x = \pi + k\pi$, where k is any integer.

(7.6) 4.   Solve the equation $(\sin^2 x - 1)(\tan x - 1) = 0$ over the interval $(0, \pi)$.

    A. $x = \pi$

    B. $x = \frac{\pi}{2}$

    C. $x = \frac{\pi}{4}$

    D. $x = \frac{\pi}{4}$ and $x = \frac{\pi}{2}$

    E. $x = \frac{\pi}{4}$, $x = \frac{\pi}{2}$, and $x = \pi$

(8.1) 5.   Two observers 15 miles apart along a straight road observe a tornado. June, who is due west of Juanita, sees it at a bearing of 25° east of north. Juanita sees the tornado at a bearing of 63° west of north. How far is the tornado from Juanita?

    A.   13.60 miles

    B.   6.81 miles

    C.   13.37 miles

    D.   6.34 miles

    E.   16.82 miles

(8.2) 6.   The lengths of the three sides of a triangle are 6 feet, 10 feet, and 13.5 feet. Find the measure of the angle formed by the 6-foot and 10-foot sides.

    A.   90°

    B.   67.33°

    C.   112.67°

    D.   140.43°

    E.   84.02°

(8.2) 7.   Find the area of triangle ABC where $a = 5$, $b = 13$, and $c = 14\frac{1}{3}$.

    A.   205.29 square units

    B.   14.33 square units

    C.   32.37 square units

    D.   32.50 square units

    E.   35.83 square units

(8.5) 8.   A plane is flying on a bearing 23° east of north at 650 mph. Express the velocity of the plane as a vector.

    A. $(598.33, 253.98)$

    B. $(253.98, 598.33)$

    C. $(0.92, 0.39)$

    D. $(-598.33, 253.98)$

    E. $(598.33, -253.98)$

(9.1) 9.   Find parametric equations for a spiral beginning at the origin.

    A. $x = t\cos t$ and $y = t\sin t$

    B. $x = t\sin t$ and $y = t\sin t$

    C. $x = 5\cos t$ and $y = 5\sin t$

    D. $x = \cos t$ and $y = \sin t$

    E. $x = t$ and $y = \sin t$

(9.3) 10.   A ball is hit with an initial velocity of 125 ft/sec at an angle of elevation of 35° and from a height of 3.5 feet. Consider the position of the ball at any time t, where $t = 0$ when the ball is hit. Neglect air resistance. Find the horizontal distance the ball will travel.

    A.   221.05 feet

    B.   84.13 feet

    C.   458.73 feet

    D.   293.31 feet

    E.   463.84 feet

(9.4) 11.   Find the length of the major axis of the elipse $49x^2 - 294x + 25y^2 + 150y - 559 = 0$.

    A.   7

    B.   14

    C.   10

    D.   25

    E.   49

(9.4) 12.   Which equation is that of the parabola that passes through the points $(3, 5)$ and $(6, 9)$?

    A. $y = \dfrac{4}{27}x^2 + \dfrac{11}{3}$

    B. $y = \dfrac{4}{27}x^2 + \dfrac{15}{4}$

    C. $y = \dfrac{27}{4}x^2 - \dfrac{3}{4}$

    D. $4y = 27x^2 - 9$

    E. $108y = 4x^2 + 15$

(10.1) 13.   Find the simultaneous solutions to the following system:

$$3x + 4y - 6z = 4$$
$$x + 2y = 8$$
$$5x + 2z = 4$$

    A. $(4, 2, 0)$

    B. $(0, 4, 2)$

    C. $(0, 0, 0)$

    D. $(0, 8, 4)$

    E. $(2, 4, 0)$

(10.3) 14.   Write a matrix equation for the following system of linear equations:

$$3x + 6y = -2$$
$$2x - 4y = 10$$

A. $\begin{pmatrix} 3 & 2 \\ 6 & -4 \end{pmatrix} \begin{pmatrix} x \\ y \end{pmatrix} = \begin{pmatrix} -2 \\ 10 \end{pmatrix}$

B. $\begin{pmatrix} 3 & 6 \\ 2 & -4 \end{pmatrix} \begin{pmatrix} x \\ y \end{pmatrix} = \begin{pmatrix} 10 \\ -2 \end{pmatrix}$

C. $\begin{pmatrix} 3 & 6 \\ 2 & -4 \end{pmatrix} \begin{pmatrix} x \\ y \end{pmatrix} = \begin{pmatrix} -2 \\ 10 \end{pmatrix}$

D. $\begin{pmatrix} -\frac{1}{4} & -\frac{1}{2} \\ -\frac{1}{6} & \frac{1}{3} \end{pmatrix} \begin{pmatrix} x \\ y \end{pmatrix} = \begin{pmatrix} -2 \\ 10 \end{pmatrix}$

E. $\begin{pmatrix} 3 & 2 \\ 6 & -4 \end{pmatrix} \begin{pmatrix} x \\ y \end{pmatrix} = \begin{pmatrix} 10 \\ -2 \end{pmatrix}$

(10.4) 15.   Give the equations that will rotate a point (x, y) through a $35°$ clockwise rotation.
A. $x' = x\cos(-35°) + y\sin(-35°)$ and $y' = x\sin(-35°) + y\sin(-35°)$
B. $x' = x\cos 35° + x\sin 35°$ and $y' = y\sin 35° + y\sin 35°$
C. $x' = x\cos 35° - y\sin 35°$ and $y' = x\sin 35° + y\sin 35°$
D. $x' = x\cos(-35°) - y\sin(-35°)$ and $y' = x\sin(-35°) + y\sin(-35°)$
E. $x' = x\sin(-35°) - y\cos(-35°)$ and $y' = x\sin(-35°) + y\sin(-35°)$

(10.5) 16.   Find the simultaneous solutions to the system

$$\frac{x^2}{2} + \frac{y^2}{5} = 1$$
$$y = \frac{1}{3}x.$$

A. $(1.38, 0.46)$
B. $(-1.38, -0.46)$
C. $(1.38, -0.46)$
D. $(-1.38, -0.46)$ and $(1.38, -0.46)$
E. $(-1.38, -0.46)$ and $(1.38, 0.46)$

(11.1) 17.   Determine the 25th term of the geometric sequence $5, 2, \dfrac{4}{5}, \dfrac{8}{25}, \dots$.

A. $\left(\dfrac{2}{5}\right)^{25}$

B. $5\left(\dfrac{2}{5}\right)^{25}$

C. $5\left(\dfrac{2}{5}\right)^{24}$

D. $5\left(\dfrac{5}{2}\right)^{24}$

E. $(5)^{25}$

(11.2) 18. Determine the fifth partial sum of the geometric sequence 2, 6, 18, 54, ...

    A.   121

    B.   242

    C.   −242

    D.   80

    E.   40

(11.3) 19. Find the seventeenth term of $(2x + 5y)^{25}$, where the leading term is considered the zeroth term.

    A. $\binom{25}{17}(2x)^8(5y)^{17}$

    B. $\binom{25}{17}(2x)^{17}(5y)^8$

    C. $\binom{25}{17}(2x)^{18}(5y)^7$

    D. $\binom{25}{17}(2x)^7(5y)^{18}$

    E. $\binom{25}{17}(2x)^{17}(5y)^{25}$

(11.6) 20. How many 6-letter computer codes can be written if no letters are repeated?

    A.   6!

    B. $_{26}P_6$

    C. $_{26}C_6$

    D.   6!26!

    E.   6!20!

(11.7) 21. Find $|\mathbf{v}|$, where $\mathbf{v}$ is the 3-space vector $(-3, 5, 2)$.

    A.   3.61

    B.   4

    C.   38

    D.   3.16

    E.   6.16

(12.1) 22. A red die and a green die are rolled. Find the probability of rolling a sum greater than 6.

    A. $\dfrac{5}{12}$

    B. $\dfrac{13}{18}$

    C. $\dfrac{7}{12}$

    D. $\dfrac{5}{36}$

    E. $\dfrac{1}{4}$

(12.2) 23. A fair coin is tossed six times. Find the probability of four or five heads occurring.

A. $\dfrac{15}{64}$

B. $\dfrac{3}{32}$

C. $\dfrac{9}{64}$

D. $\dfrac{21}{64}$

E. $\dfrac{1}{3}$

(12.3) 24. Find the mean of the data set {4.5, 5.9, 6.7, 4.3, 4.8, 5.5, 5.6, 6.1, 6.0, 5.0}.

A. 5.15

B. 5.55

C. 6.04

D. 5.44

E. 4.95

(12.4) 25. Find the standard deviation of the data set {51, 57, 43, 65, 72, 39, 56, 61, 48, 49}.

A. 3.10

B. 92.29

C. 9.61

D. 8.10

E. 9.16

End-of-Year Test–Form B

Answer Sheet

1. Answer: A B C D E
2. Answer: A B C D E
3. Answer: A B C D E
4. Answer: A B C D E
5. Answer: A B C D E
6. Answer: A B C D E
7. Answer: A B C D E
8. Answer: A B C D E
9. Answer: A B C D E
10. Answer: A B C D E
11. Answer: A B C D E
12. Answer: A B C D E
13. Answer: A B C D E
14. Answer: A B C D E
15. Answer: A B C D E
16. Answer: A B C D E
17. Answer: A B C D E
18. Answer: A B C D E
19. Answer: A B C D E
20. Answer: A B C D E
21. Answer: A B C D E
22. Answer: A B C D E
23. Answer: A B C D E
24. Answer: A B C D E
25. Answer: A B C D E